David K. Sauer

David Mamet's
Oleanna

continuum

Continuum International Publishing Group

The Tower Building   80 Maiden Lane
11 York Road   Suite 704, New York
London SE1 7NX   NY 10038

www.continuumbooks.com

British Library Cataloguing-in-Publication Data
A catalogue record for this book is available from the British Library.

ISBN: 978-08264-9645-4 (hardback)
        978-0-8264-9646-1 (paperback)

Library of Congress Cataloging-in-Publication Data
A catalog record for this book is available from the Library of Congress.

Contents

Acknowledgements

As always my greatest debt is to my spouse of forty years, Jan, whose excellence is not limited to her professional skills of reference, and proofing, but includes attending productions, reading criticism, and working with me every step of the way. In addition, her scepticism about Mamet's views on acting and directing has been a continuing source of perspective. My son Geoffrey's contribution has informed all my work in theory and he has fought through these issues with me with great patience. For 35 years I have also worked with Michael Kaffer and John Hafner at Spring Hill College – no one could ask for more generous, thoughtful and stimulating colleagues. All three of us studied with Howard Stein whose enthusiasm for American Drama was contagious. In addition, Michael and Brianne Bordes worked with me for a semester on a production of *Oleanna*, to help me understand the play from the inside – both also attended other productions with me and are fearless in their approach to Mamet. Finally, Nan Altmayer provided generous financial support for our Department and the College endowing a rotating chair that allowed us to deepen our approaches to dramatic literature.

Every year for the past twelve I have gone to the New York Public Library Performing Arts Branch at Lincoln Center which is an invaluable resource both in its clippings files and in the videotape archival holdings, as of Mamet's original production of *Oleanna*. In London the Theatre Museum similarly has a most useful video of Pinter's London production of the play. And assisting me through the process of writing I am most grateful to my editor, Aleks Sierz for his help, modelling, and encouragement; and at Continuum, Colleen Coalter for her support. Finally, I am indebted to Bill Macy and Debra Eisenstadt for appearing at David Mamet Society sessions and generously spending time with me discussing the production.

Extracts from *Oleanna* by David Mamet, copyright © 1992 by David Mamet. Used by permission of Pantheon Books, a division of Random House Inc. Permission to use extracts from *Oleanna* by David Mamet have also been granted by Methuen Drama, an imprint of A&C Black Publishers.

DAVID K. SAUER
Mobile, AL
March 2008

General Preface

Continuum Modern Theatre Guides

Volumes in the series *Continuum Modern Theatre Guides* offer concise and informed introductions to the key plays of modern times. Each book takes a close look at one particular play's dramaturgical qualities and then at its various theatrical manifestations. The books are carefully structured to offer a systematic study of the play in its biographical, historical, social and political context, followed by an in-depth study of the text and a chapter which outlines the work's production history, examining both the original productions of the play and subsequent major stage interpretations. Where relevant, screen adaptations will also be analyzed. There then follows a chapter dedicated to workshopping the play, based on suggested group exercises. Also included are a timeline and suggestions for further reading.

Each book covers:

- Background and context
- Analysis of the play
- Production history
- Workshopping exercises

The aim is to provide accessible introductions to modern plays for students in both Theatre/Performance Studies and English, as well as for informed general readers. The series includes up-to-date coverage of a broad range of key plays, with summaries of important critical approaches and the intellectual debates that have illuminated the meaning of the work and made a significant contribution to our broader cultural life. They will enable readers to develop their understanding of playwrights and theatre-makers, as well as inspiring them to broaden their studies.

The Editors:
Steve Barfield, Janelle Reinelt,
Graham Saunders and Aleks Sierz
March 2008

1 Background and Context

This chapter is an introduction to the study of David Mamet's *Oleanna* (1992). It explains why the play is important, gives a sketch of its author's life and discusses the social, economic and political background to the play.

Introduction: the significance of *Oleanna*

> Experiencing David Mamet's play 'Oleanna' on the stage was one of the most stimulating experiences I've had in a theater. In two acts, he succeeded in enraging all of the audience – the women with the first act, the men with the second. I recall loud arguments breaking out during the intermission and after the play, as the audience spilled out of an off Broadway theater all worked up over its portrait of . . . sexual harassment? Or was it self-righteous Political Correctness? (Ebert, 1994)

Oleanna has established its noteworthiness because, like other landmarks of modern drama *A Doll's House*, *Playboy of the Western World*, and *Pygmalion*, it set off a firestorm of controversy in the wake of its initial productions both in the US and Britain. *Oleanna's* controversies share similarities with those plays' issues – gender, national identity, as well as proscribed language. Combining these, *Oleanna* proved an explosive package in its time, and continues to be so today where performances are often followed by extended audience discussions on the issues the play raises, and the differing perceptions audience members have about the play and performance.

Those earlier plays were crafted by playwrights who were critics of society, and who knew what was wrong with their cultures. *Oleanna's* importance in the history of drama arises from its role as an exemplar of a new kind of drama, 'postmodern realism', designed to engender controversy over issues for which the playwright has no solution. At first it appears to be a conventionally realistic play, but proves itself in the end to be unconventional. Rather, it is a Rorschach play – like an inkblot in which different viewers see very different things. *Oleanna* creates an experience, which deepens with discussion afterwards. Because of the apparent realistic style, audiences think that what they've seen is real – yet in discussion it emerges that they often have opposing points of view. And each side is usually convinced it is right, and can't understand the other, as Mamet explains to Charlie Rose:

> Well, I heard from most people, many people thought that the, the balance of power or the balance of rectitude, if you will – [. . .] between the two protagonists was lopsided. But they didn't always think that the same person was on top. A lot of people thought that the, the [*sic*] man was right and the woman was wrong and that I'd slanted it that way, and a lot of people thought the opposite. And that's why the people were slapping each other around in the lobby because they each, the audience each thought, or the members of the audience vehemently believed, that their hero in the play was correct and that the other person's hero was wrong. (Rose, 1994: 164–5)

As a result, *Oleanna* achieved notoriety in the wake of its initial productions both in the US and Britain. The *Oleanna* controversy encompasses issues of political correctness, of gender conflict, of views of power and sexism.

Arthur Holmberg reported on the outraged reaction in Cambridge, Massachusetts, to the initial production: 'Mamet was attacked by people on both sides of the sexual battlefront. "Your play is politically irresponsible," one female student challenged the playwright. "You don't take a position. Your political statement is wrong." . . . "As a playwright", Mamet answered, "I have no political responsibility. I'm an artist. I write plays, not political propaganda. If you want easy solutions, turn on the boob tube. Social and political issues on TV are cartoons; the good guy wears a white hat, the bad guy a black hat. Cartoons don't interest me. We are living through a time of deep transition, so everyone is unsettled. I'm as angry, scared, and confused as the rest of you. I don't have the answers" ' (Holmberg, 1992: 94). When *Oleanna* moved to New York, it similarly inflamed audiences. Mamet recounted to Charlie Rose his play's response: 'It first frightened me because I'd never imagined that kind of reaction to this play. People used to get into literally fistfights with each other in, in the lobby, and screaming matches and going home . . .' (Rose, 1994: 164).

Even more curiously, William H. Macy, who starred as John, told me that after each performance, when people came backstage to congratulate the actors, they tended to snub Rebecca Pidgeon who played Carol. It was a strange reaction – they didn't see Pidgeon, they saw Carol, and wanted nothing to do with her. Pidgeon's understudy in New York was Debra Eisenstadt, and she spoke with Liane Hansen about the unprecedented reaction to the ending of the play, both to her character and to herself:

Oh, yeah. Here, they've been cheering [during the final scene]. And it's a little disconcerting that anyone would cheer when someone's getting beaten on stage. I mean, it gets harder and harder as I do it because I know I'm getting up to the point where I'm going to say this and they're going to gasp and they're going to hate me even more and then I'm going to get – then they're going to cheer, and they're going to clap and they're going to you [k]now, and it's hard, but you just have to you know, throw it out the window and say, 'listen, this is not me.' This is what I'm playing. [. . .] Because they don't like me. (Hansen, 1993)

This passage is the clearest account of the bizarre nature of this play. For one thing, when I saw this production, it was a matinee with mainly older women, and they were the ones who applauded. Initial reports were that it was men who applauded, but as Eisenstadt indicates, it was not a gendered response. Some women were as threatened in their roles by this kind of late twentieth-century New Woman as some men. Secondly, she confirms Macy's account that audiences cheer, but also do something unprecedented – they dislike not only the character, but the actor as well.

At an MLA session on Performance in the late 1990s, a panellist told me that at her California university a performance was stopped when a female professor jumped up during the production to yell at the student actor playing Carol, 'You should not be doing this play.' People enter into the play so completely that they forget it is theatre, or that what they've seen is as much a mirror as an alternate reality.

Oleanna is extraordinary as well because, unlike any other play, there is a record of the audience response. When Mamet took the production to Washington DC's Kennedy Center with Macy and Eisenstadt (they are the film cast as well), the management put a gigantic blackboard out in the lobby where ushers recorded votes. As the audience left the theatre they were asked: 'Is he right?' said one column, 'Could it really happen?' said another, and 'Was she wronged?' asked the third. Megan Rosenfeld wrote up the results of the poll for the *Washington Post*:

Tuesday night's results were noticeably different from the rest of the week's – perhaps because there were more young people, perhaps because the reviews had appeared the day before. On Tuesday, 61 percent of those who voted thought he was right, compared with a week-long average of 79 percent. Thirty-nine percent thought she was wronged, compared with the average of 21 percent. And only 85 percent said something like this could really happen, compared with the normal 96 percent. But get this: At last Saturday's matinee, traditionally the show of choice for older women, people who don't like to go out at night and those seeking cheaper seats, a whopping 81 percent thought he was right, and 100 percent said it could really happen. That audience also cheered the loudest when he slammed her at the end, according to a theater manager. (Rosenfeld, 1993)

The last line is the most shocking, and mirrored both my experience at the same theatre and reports of the New York audience often breaking out in cheers or applause at the end of the play when the professor beats up the student. Clearly something extraordinary takes place in the audience of *Oleanna* that breaks down the usual reserve of audiences and allows them to voice feelings during the production. Moreover, they cheer an act which in any other context would be repugnant.

Unlike modernist experimenters such as Ibsen and Miller, Mamet is significant because his postmodern minimalism leaves so much of interpretation open to the viewer. This style coincides perfectly with the message of *Oleanna* which deals with the issue of differing perceptions of the same event. After I saw the first act of the play in Washington, and went out into the lobby, I reflected on what a bland play it was – how could it have provoked so much antipathy and anger in New York? The first act I saw was almost innocuous – and it was hard to imagine how the remaining half of the play could possibly ignite any kind of fire. When I came in for the second act, and realized that Carol was filing her claim based entirely on what I just saw in the first act, I was astounded. But by the end of the performance I had not only come to understand her perspective, but to see the play from within that point of view.

I voted 'She was wronged' and realized I had misread the whole first act initially.

The play's minimal construction is another key to its significance as well as a reason for its success in engendering controversy: it is a two-hander with almost no set other than desk, bench and chairs. As a result, audiences seem to inject themselves into the play to fill in the gaps and spaces, and as a consequence become more than passive observers. The play they witness is partially constructed by them, and therefore no two people see exactly the same play. Mamet's construction of the play is as innovative as the issues it brings to consciousness.

That Mamet had this end in view early in his career is evident in the essay 'A National Dream-Life' (1978) which argues that 'We respond to a drama to that extent to which it corresponds to our dream life. The life of the play is the life of the unconscious, the protagonist represents ourselves, and the main action of the play constitutes the subject of the dream or myth' (Mamet, 1986: 8). The play thus reveals what the nation represses, and the playwright's unconscious engages 'the public as a whole, and as a *community endeavor*'; the result is that 'the artistic community (subconsciously) elects and forms our national dreams' (Mamet, 1986: 10).

Mamet achieved this elevated purpose in the 1970s with his tale of a failed burglary, *American Buffalo* (1976), which Robert Vorlicky observes reflected the Watergate break-in. Similarly *Glengarry Glen Ross* (1983) exposed the capitalism-gone-mad, me-decade of the 1980s. In 1992 *Oleanna* revealed national fears about empowerment of women, political correctness and gender (in)equality in the same way.

In a subsequent essay included in *Writing in Restaurants*, 'Radio Drama', Mamet argues that 'The best production takes place in the mind of the beholder' (Mamet, 1986: 16). James Dishon McDermott amplifies the point to explain how Mamet's plays work on an audience: 'Mamet himself, however, sees his works not as naturalistic texts that match fictive action to a precise, unchanging reality but as coded yet open-ended texts that – in their lack of inflection – compel the audience to project its desires and anxieties onto the characters and events depicted on the stage' (McDermott, 2006: 115).

The key to the play in performance is not which side one chooses, but the recognition of divided response through the sounds the audience makes when the beating begins. As a result one suddenly realizes that Mamet was right, and that we have grown used to plays which tell us which side to choose: 'We leave the theater after such plays as smug as after a satisfying daydream. Our prejudices have been assuaged, and we have been reassured that nothing is wrong, but we are, finally, no happier' (Mamet, 1986: 10). At the end of *Oleanna*, however, one still feels that one's own view is right, but the theatrical experience, because of audible reactions, reveals that other people, regardless of which side one chooses, respond in diverse ways.

As a consequence, one must ultimately recognize that the issue is not who is right and who is wrong, but rather – why do we come to such different responses? Within the play, Carol makes the point – 'You think, you think you can deny that these things happened; or, if they *did*, if they *did*, that they meant what you *said* they meant. Don't you see?' (48). Her point is exactly right – who is right and wrong is not a matter of intention; meaning is determined, at least in the postmodern decentred world of global capitalism, by who has the power; there is no more agreement on who is right and who is wrong.

About David Mamet

While it is always tempting to draw connections between real life events and his plays, Mamet puts a distance between his personal life and experiences and his professional life. Unlike O'Neill, Miller or Williams, most of his plays deal with workplace issues rather than with home and family: *American Buffalo* (1975), *A Life in the Theatre* (1977), *The Water Engine* (1977), *Lakeboat* (1980), *Glengarry Glen Ross* (1983), *Speed-the-Plow* (1988), *Oleanna* (1992), *Romance* (2005). After *Oleanna*, Mamet turns to more autobiographical subject matter about marriage, *The Cryptogram* (1994) and *The Old Neighborhood* (1997).

David Mamet was born on 30 November 1947, in Chicago, the son of attorney Bernard Morris and teacher Lenore June, née Silver. He remembers growing up in an ethnic neighbourhood of Chicago where his grandmother 'spoke in what could have been Yiddish, Polish or Russian' to the shopkeepers; they lived on Euclid Avenue, and his grandparents were Ashkenazi Jews from Poland (*The Cabin*, 1992: 125–8). He went to Parkside School where he recalls those days in 'When I was Young – A Note to Zosia and Willa' (*Some Freaks*, 1989: 154–7) where he remembers the stickball played in the street; in *The Old Neighborhood* Bob Gould recollects similar games in Chicago with a childhood friend. Mamet discovered acting through his Uncle Henry who 'was a producer of radio and television for the Chicago Board of Rabbis. And he gave me jobs as a kid and my sister jobs as a kid, portraying Jewish children on television and radio. And through him I got into community theater in Chicago' (Shulgasser, 1998: 196).

Mamet's awareness of language he sometimes attributes to his attorney-father, but many commentators think his distinctive style of dialogue is rooted in Chicago ways of speaking – as the *Chicago Sun-Times* puts it: 'Mamet's distinctive, clipped, rhythmic, singularly visceral style continues to suggest he found much inspiration for his unique writing in the no-nonsense, gritty, all-American urban world of Chicago' (Lazare, 2007: 59).

His mother and father divorced in 1958, and when his mother remarried, they moved to a Chicago suburb amidst the cornfields where he described the psychological and physical abuse of his sister and, as he later discovered, of his mother when she was a girl (*The Cabin*, 1992: 3–11). 'Jolly', the second act of *The Old Neighborhood*, depicts a similar story, recollecting childhood abuse and resentments particularly after a divorce and the introduction of stepfather, stepbrother and sister.

In high school he 'hung around Second City [Chicago's renowned improvisation troupe] quite a bit,' working there as a busboy, and later, in tribute to its stars, lived as they had at 'The Hotel Lincoln' (*The Cabin*, 1992: 95–9). In the mid 1960s, after graduation from high school, he worked in a factory, living on the North side near Addison Avenue, and commuting to work near Cicero (on the western border of Chicago) where he worked welding, and spraying weeds around the building and in maintenance, tearing out asbestos ceilings to which he attributed years of weak lungs, 'which seems to me a more dramatic story than 25 years of tobacco' (*The Cabin*, 1992: 77–81). He also drove a cab in Chicago (*Jafsie and John Henry*, 1999: 17–19). He claims that the style of his earliest plays, *Sexual Perversity in Chicago*, *Duck Variations* and *Lakeboat*, all written in short scenes, reflects Second City where short skits with blackouts for endings were the norm.

In 1965, Mamet worked at a roadside diner in Trois-Rivières, Province de Quebec. In an essay he also described working in 1967 at Montreal's Expo '67 as an 'acro dancer' in a Maurice Chevalier show, *Toutes voiles dehors*!!! (*The Cabin*, 1992: 25–30) and then went to Goddard, an experimental college in Vermont. In his twentieth year Mamet studied at the Neighborhood Playhouse School of Sanford Meisner in New York City as a 'study abroad' experience (*Writing in Restaurants*, 1986: 19–23). There he learned two first principles to which he devoted himself as he recalls in the preface to *Writing in Restaurants*: '(1) every aspect of the production should reflect the idea of the play; (2) the purpose of the play is to bring to the stage the life of the soul' (viii). In 1969 he was graduated from Goddard with a BA degree.

After college he lived at 71st and Columbus Circle in New York City and worked 'as an usher, then house manager, then assistant stage manager for *The Fantasticks*' ('Salad Days', 1999: 8). In the summer he got a job in 'summer stock out on the tip of Long Island, and it may have been the only time, or at least one of the few times, I was ever hired as an actor' ('Salad Days', 1999: 9). In 1970 he became a special lecturer in drama at Marlboro College, replacing an acting teacher who was on sabbatical and where *Lakeboat* was first produced. Afterwards, Mamet returned to Chicago where he sold real estate 'to unsuspecting elderly people' (Zweigler, 1976: 17).

In 1971–72 he was artist-in-residence in drama at Goddard where one of his courses was an experiment in team-teaching a Shakespeare course with poet Barry Goldensohn. Mamet taught the theatrical approach; Goldensohn the poetic. While at Goddard he formed the St. Nicholas Theater Company with students William H. Macy and Steven Schachter who performed the first versions of *Duck Variations* and *Sexual Perversity in Chicago*.

In 1972 he returned to Chicago. *Duck Variations* and *Litko* were performed at the Body Politic Theatre. By 1974 *Sexual Perversity in Chicago* was also done by the Organic Theater Company, and won Chicago's Joe Jefferson Award. Mamet revived the St. Nicholas Theater Company there and on 10 October premiered *Squirrels*. 'The Company is named for Nicholas of Maya, Patron of mountebanks, prostitutes and the *demi-monde*.' These notes from the program also included the Company's purpose: 'Using Stanislavsky's definition that "Acting is living truthfully under imaginary circumstances," we have worked to establish a common vocabulary, and a common method which will permit us to bring to the stage (not through our insights, but through our craft) this truth in the form of *action*.' In 'Stanislavsky and Squirrels' in the *Chicago Sun-Times* on 6 October 1974, Mamet amplified, 'the philosophy that life on the stage is not an imitation of anything, but is real life on the stage.' *Oleanna* reflects this view, misleading audiences into taking it as real life, voting overwhelmingly, that it could 'really happen'.

In 1975 Gregory Mosher directed *American Buffalo* at the Goodman Theatre's Stage 2. The production moved to St. Nicholas Theater on Halsted Street. *Sexual Perversity* and *Duck Variations* opened off-off Broadway at the St. Clement's Theatre in New York, and won an Obie for best new play. Mamet then wrote *Revenge of the Space Pandas* for St. Clement's. He also wrote *Marranos* and *Mackinac* for Youth Theater of the Bernard Horwich Jewish Community Center in Chicago.

In 1976 he lived in New York which he describes in 'Memories of Chelsea' (*The Cabin*, 1992: 13–23). Mamet's big impact occurred during 1976–77 when productions hit New York in quick succession. Mosher's production of *American Buffalo* came to St. Clement's in New York in January, 1976, and won an Obie and earlier Chicago's Joe Jefferson. *Sexual Perversity* and *Duck Variations* moved to the Cherry Lane in June, 1976. In an interview Mamet explained: 'Voltaire said words were invented to hide feelings. That's what the play is about, how what we say influences what we think. The words that the old Bernie Litko says to Danny influences his behavior, you know, that women are broads, that they're there to exploit.' Instead of characters having thoughts which require words, the order is reversed into postmodernism: 'that words create behavior' (Fraser, 1976: 11). Words define the kinds of thoughts that are possible.

Ulu Grosbard directed *American Buffalo* with Robert Duvall on Broadway in February 1977, winning a New York Drama Critics' Circle Award. Meantime, *A Life in the Theatre* opened in Chicago at the Goodman Stage 2, and moved to the Théâtre de Lys in New York. In May, the St. Nicholas Theater in Chicago staged *The Water Engine,* while *Reunion* and *Dark Pony* premiered at the Yale Repertory Theatre, *Revenge of the Space Pandas* was staged at the St. Nicholas and Flushing Town Hall, Queens. *Sexual Perversity in Chicago* and *Duck Variations* were performed in London at the

Regent's Theatre. In November, Mamet directed Peter Weller and Patti LuPone at the St. Nicholas Theater in *The Woods*. In December of 1977, Mamet married actor Lindsay Crouse.

In 1978 *Water Engine* aired on Earplay, National Public Radio, as did *Prairie du Chien*. From the experience Mamet writes he became a better playwright: 'More than any other medium it teaches the writer to concentrate on the essentials, because it throws into immediate relief that to *characterize* the people or scene is to take time from the story – to weaken the story' (*Writing in Restaurants* 14). In January of 1978 the Public Theater in New York staged *The Water Engine*; it then moved to Broadway's Plymouth Theatre. In 1979, the Public Theater also staged *The Blue Hour: City Sketches* and *The Woods* in 1978. A musical, *Lone Canoe, or the Explorer* was unsuccessful at the Goodman. PBS television aired *A Life in the Theatre*. Mamet directed *Reunion and Dark Pony* at the Circle in the Square in 1979. A fascinating videotape exists of his directing of Crouse and Michael Higgins in these plays: *David Mamet: The Playwright as Director*. It is the best introduction to the Mamet method.

In 1980, Mamet reworked *Lakeboat* for the Milwaukee Repertory Theatre. The Long Wharf Theatre redid *American Buffalo* with Al Pacino as Teach, transferring to Circle in the Square in 1981, and was revived on Broadway in 1983. The same production also showed at London's Duke of York's Theatre in August of 1984. During this time Mamet bought a farmhouse and cabin on one hundred acres in Cabot, Vermont for fifty thousand dollars and did much of his writing there for the next twenty years (*South of the Northeast Kingdom*, 2002: 84).

Mamet turned to film in 1981, writing his first screenplay for a remake of James M. Cain's *The Postman Always Rings Twice*. He also worked on a script for *The Verdict* for which he received an Academy Award nomination in 1982. In that year as well, Mamet's *Lakeboat* was produced at both Long Wharf and the Goodman, and *Edmond* premiered at the Goodman, then went to New York where it received an Obie, Off-Broadway's Award.

Chicago's Goodman Theatre was the site of his adaptation *Red River* and 'The Disappearance of the Jews' an one-act done with plays by Elaine May and Shel Silverstein. He sent the script of *Glengarry Glen Ross* to Harold Pinter asking for advice, and Pinter said simply – 'stage it' (*New York Times* 24 February 1984: C2). So Pinter sent it to the National Theatre which mounted a production that won both an Olivier and Society of West End Theatres' Award. In 1984 Mosher directed a production with an American cast at the Goodman, and then moved it to Broadway where it won the Pulitzer Prize, Drama Critics' Award for Best Play, and four Tony Nominations. Mamet described his job to Mel Gussow in this play 'to create a closed moral universe, and to leave evaluation to the audience' (*New York Times* 28 Mar. 1984: C19).

When Henry Schvey asks him about sympathy for Roma in that play, Mamet replies, 'I always want everyone to be sympathetic to all the characters. Because when you aren't, what you are doing is writing a melodrama with good guys and bad guys. Drama is really about the conflicting impulses in the individual. That is what all drama is about' (Schvey, 1988: 65).

In 1985–86 Mamet's one-acts were staged in various venues – *The Shawl* and *Prairie du Chien* reopened the Lincoln Center Theatre for which Mosher became artistic director. In 1985 Mamet's adaptation of Chekhov's *The Cherry Orchard* appeared at the New Theatre Company, which he founded in New York with Mosher. Mamet's first collection of essays also appeared in 1986 – *Writing in Restaurants*. And the following year, Mamet did the screenplay for *The Untouchables* and wrote and directed his first film, *House of Games*. In *On Directing Film*, lectures he gave at Columbia in 1987, he proposes that 'the only thing I know about film directing' is Eisenstein's theory of montage. Rather than following a character around with a camera, Mamet's method is '*a succession of images*

*juxtaposed so that the contrast between these images moves the story for-
ward in the mind of the audience'* (2). Like the blackout method of
his early plays, *Lakeboat, Sexual Perversity in Chicago,* and *Duck
Variations,* this approach asked the audience to make the connections, rather than making them for the audience. In 1988 the
second film he wrote (with Shel Silverstein) and directed, *Things
Change,* was released, and the American Repertory Theatre debuted
his adaptation of *Uncle Vanya.*

In 1988 *Speed-the-Plow* premiered on Broadway to great acclaim
and controversy. Joe Mantegna and Ron Silver were nominated for
Tonys for their performances. In 1989 the play moved to the
National Theatre with similar acclaim and more positive reviews of
Rebecca Pidgeon as Karen. Macy and Mamet had founded The
Atlantic Theatre Company in 1985 and did Mamet's adaptation of
Three Sisters in 1990. Mamet divorced Crouse in 1990 – they have
two children, Willa and Zosia.

Mamet wrote and directed *Homicide* in 1991 and married
Rebecca Pidgeon. She starred with Macy in *Oleanna* which Mamet
directed in 1992 at the American Repertory Theatre at Harvard,
and then moved to the Orpheum Theater in New York. In 1993
Harold Pinter directed the play in London with an added ending
from an earlier draft. In 1994 Mamet wrote and directed the
film version of the play with Macy and Eisenstadt who replaced
Pidgeon, pregnant with their first child, Clara. His screenplay of
Hoffa was also made into a film in 1992.

In that year Mamet's screenplay for *Glengarry Glen Ross* was
filmed with an all-star cast directed by James Foley. Also André
Gregory's film *Vanya on 42nd Street* was made using Mamet's
adaptation. In London, Sam Mendes directed a revival of *Glengarry*
at the Donmar Warehouse to great reviews.

In 1994 Greg Mosher directed the premier of *Cryptogram* at
Ambassadors Theatre London. In 1995 Mamet directed the play in
Boston and later Westside Theatre in New York. In the same year,

his one-act 'An Interview' appeared in *Death Defying Acts* with plays by Woody Allen and Elaine May. Mamet directed J. B. Priestley's *Dangerous Corner* for the Atlantic Theatre Company.

The same company revived *Edmond* in 1996. Ensemble Theater did two one-acts of Mamet's, and the film of *American Buffalo* was released. Mamet put together three of his one-acts into *The Old Neighborhood* in 1997 at American Repertory Theatre. The production then moved to Booth Theatre, New York City with Patti LuPone and Peter Riegert; both featured Pidgeon as Deeny. The same year Mamet's screenplays for *The Edge* and adaptation of *Wag the Dog* were released, as was *The Spanish Prisoner* which he also directed.

The Old Neighborhood in 1998 debuted at the Royal Court in London with Colin Stinton and Zoë Wanamaker. The film of Mamet's screenplay *Ronin* was released and so was his adaptation of *The Winslow Boy*, also directed by Mamet. He also co-produced the HBO production of his screenplay *Lansky*.

In 1999 Mamet directed *Boston Marriage* at American Repertory Theatre and also directed and wrote the film *State and Main*. *Lakeboat*, directed by Joe Mantegna, was released in 2000. Mamet wrote and directed the popular film *Heist* in 2001. *Boston Marriage* was done at the Donmar in London in 2001. It came to New York to the Public Theater in 2002, when the Mamets moved to Los Angeles from New England. He was inducted into the Theatre Hall of Fame on January 27, 2003. In that year as well he wrote and directed *Spartan*. In February, 2004 *Faustus* appeared in San Francisco, and *Romance* in 2005 at the Atlantic. In all of these recent plays, Mamet seems to be experimenting with genre: Oscar Wilde comedy in a lesbian relationship, Renaissance tragedy, courtroom farce in theatre; thieves, screwball comedy, and then spies in the films. In 2005 Mamet also created a television series about paramilitary group called *The Unit* for CBS. In summer of 2007 *Redbelt*, directed and written by Mamet, was being filmed in 2008. In 2008 his next play, a political drama about the presidency, *November*, was the first Mamet play to debut on Broadway.

The social, political and historical context

Contemporary drama arises in the wake of postmodernism, the world view as explained by Lyotard in *The Postmodern Condition*, in which there are no successful overarching grand stories attempting to explain the world with religious or political models. The nineteenth-century progress narrative, that things are getting better and better, 'evolving', for example, has broken down. No single unifying story can connect a majority into one view of the world. Frederic Jameson amplifies the idea with an explanation that from the 1950s late capitalism has become increasingly global. At the same time, air travel and television have brought people into a much larger, multivalent world than they previously knew. And the middle class, in unprecedented numbers, began going away from home to universities. All of this brings people increasingly into contact with conflicting viewpoints and multiple contexts from which to understand each issue.

John, seemingly a professor of higher education, begins a critique of this explosion of students – 'Well, then, what is higher education? It is something-other-than-useful. [. . .] It has become a ritual, it has become an article of faith. That all must be subjected to, or to put it differently, that all are entitled to Higher Education' (28). This is his essential point which offends Carol: 'How can you say in a class. Say in a college class, that college education is a prejudice?' (31). She later amplifies that she has made great sacrifices to come to the university, while he teaches that higher education is useless. He contends most students come because of a cultural bias which makes it the gateway to the middle class, that world to which he aspires with the purchase of a house. She rebukes him: 'you mock us. You call education "hazing", and from your so-protected, so-elitist seat you hold our confusion as a *joke*, and our hopes and efforts with it' (52). It is this attack on her middle class aspirations which so offends Carol, and her threat to his similar aspirations that so upsets John. But the underlying issue is whether all students should go, and whether higher education is really of any use to most of them: 'I say college education, since the war, has become so a matter of course, and such a fashionable necessity, for those either of or aspiring *to* the new vast middle class, that we *espouse* it, as a matter of right, and have ceased to ask, "What is it good for?" ' (33).

But the very explosion of attendance at universities after World War II is part of the cause for the postmodern questioning of formerly widely accepted ideas, accepted because only the elite went to college and were in much more agreement than when students of all different backgrounds are brought together. Linda Hutcheon defines the situation:

> [Postmodernism] is neither uncertain nor suspending of judgment: it questions the very bases of any certainty (history, subjectivity, reference) and of any standards of judgment. Who sets them? When? Where? Why? Postmodernism marks less a negative 'disintegration' of or 'decline in order and coherence' (Kahler 1968) than a challenging of the very concept upon which we judge order and coherence. (Hutcheon, 1988: 57)

The lack of a single agreed upon standard, a *grand recit* in Lyotard's terms, results in this questioning of all the previously accepted assumptions. That is what John is doing in questioning the very efficacy of higher education itself, and is reflected in his view that 'We can only interpret the behavior of other through the screen we [. . .] create' (19–20).

The consequence of this change in student population is that one can no longer predicate a centre from which the periphery could be judged, as was possible with a male-only upper-class, higher-educated elite (reflected in John's patriarchal rhetoric of 'father' and 'son,' a hypothetical student as 'he', the Tenure Committee as 'good men and true' though one of the members is a woman, and 'the white man's burden'). Defining a culture in terms of difference instantly decentres the idea of a unified culture. And interpretation becomes much more difficult when there is no single agreed upon standard or point of view.

The result of this decentring is continual conflict among groups, particularly at American universities, resulting in the conflicts between 'free speech', protected by the First Amendment of the US Constitution, and what Benno Schmidt, President of Yale University, described in 1991 as 'well-intentioned but misguided efforts to give values of community and harmony a higher place than freedom' (Fish, 1992: 239). The debate raged in the early nineties, and continues today. For example, in 2007 Don Imus, pre-eminent national radio/TV morning talk show host was fired after referring to the Rutgers Women's Basketball team, playing in the NCAA championship, 'nappy-headed ho's'.

The problem of patriarchal privilege is epitomized at the convention of 'The Tailhook Association', an assembly of US Navy pilots, especially of aircraft carrier pilots. Four thousand of them met at a symposium in Las Vegas on Operation Desert Storm [Kuwait] in September of 1991. Eighty-three women and seven men stated that they had been victims of assault and sexual harassment during the meeting, according to a Department of Defense report. This scandal forms part of the background to this play, for it was the first time that a large number of women had, together, reported the sexual misconduct of men from the military. It laid a foundation in the popular imagination for such charges to be brought against men in power, as Carol does with John.

Even more of a national scandal illuminates the postmodern predicament. On October 11, 1991, Anita Hill was summoned to testify before the Senate Judiciary Committee which was holding hearings on the confirmation of Clarence Thomas to the US Supreme Court. Staffers had leaked Hill's name and she was required to testify about dealings she had when she served at the Equal Opportunity Employment Commission which was then headed by Clarence Thomas. She reported a number of inappropriate remarks made by Thomas, and was grilled for seven hours continuously, broadcast on network television to a nation for which the issue of sexual harassment was displayed for all to see.

SENATOR HEFLIN: In other words, you are basically stating that that appeared to be his goal, rather than trying to obtain an intimate or sexual relations with you. It may be that you also felt that, though that raises quite an issue. 'However, I sense that my discomfort with his discussions only urged him on as though my reaction of feeling ill at ease and vulnerable was what he wanted.' What do you mean by that? How do you conclude that?

MS. HILL: Well, it was almost as though he wanted me at a disadvantage, to put me at a disadvantage, so that I would have to concede to whatever his wishes were.

SENATOR HEFLIN: Do you think that he got some pleasure out of seeing you ill at ease and vulnerable?

MS. HILL: I think so, yes.

SENATOR HEFLIN: Was this feeling more so than a feeling that he might be seeking some type of dating or social relationship with you?

MS. HILL: I think it was as combination of factors. I think that he wanted to see me vulnerable and that, if I were vulnerable, then he could extract from me whatever he wanted, whether it was sexual or otherwise, that I would be under his control. (Committee, 1991: 88)

This excerpt of Senator Heflin's questioning makes clear the difficulties of such accusations. To Senator Heflin, it is not precisely clear what Clarence Thomas actually sought, if it was not simply a sexual relationship.

In 1991, public opinion polls showed that 47 per cent of those polled believed Thomas, while only 24 per cent believed Hill. By 1992 those numbers had reversed: 44 per cent believed Hill and only 34 per cent believed Thomas (*New York Times* 5 October 1992: 1). The key point, however, was that the spectre of an all-male Senate committee grilling Anita Hill was dismaying and appeared unfair and insensitive. The next election saw the greatest turnover of men and election of women in House and Senate. The sentiment in the country was that the men 'just don't get it', and numerous polls revealed that large numbers of American women felt they had been similarly harassed.

The crux of the matter, however, was that revealed by Mamet's play – in a two-person confrontation, each might see the events totally differently. And so will the outside observers, as the poll numbers show. Again, as Mamet's play so rightly asserts, 'We can only interpret the behavior of other through the screen we [. . .] create' (19–20). The precedent was cited when *Oleanna* debuted, Bruce Weber citing Mamet: ' "The first draft", he said, "was written some eight months before the Hill-Thomas hearings, but it was the hearings that led him to pull it out of a drawer and work on it again" ' (C2).

One final consequence of the postmodern shift is that the view of education has changed from the Enlightenment concept of learning the material to the postmodern view that what one must learn are not answers, but how to pose the questions. The different theories of education which John teaches deal with this postmodern idea of seeing truth from a variety of perspectives.

This concept was revealed in the foundational work on how college students learn, William G. Perry Jr.'s (1970) *Forms of Intellectual and Moral Development in the College Years: A Scheme*. Based on extensive interviews with Harvard students, Perry sketches a series of nine stages of intellectual development which are relevant to understanding the initial conflicts of Carol and John. Like Perry's college student at the initial stage, Carol is in a state of 'dualism' in which she sees answers as either right or wrong. This kind of student, according to Perry, thinks the teacher has all the right answers, and the student's job is simply to get them, write them down, and learn them: 'I did what you told me. I did, I did everything that, I read your book, you told me to buy your book and read it. Everything you say I . . . (*She gestures to her notebook*)' (9). Since she has done all that she thinks is in the student contract, she is completely frustrated because she followed the rules, she 'did everything' that he said, she writes it all down in the notebook, and yet this does not result in her excelling in the course, but in failing.

College students, according to Perry, move out of this stage quickly to a view that sees a multiplicity of possible answers, 'everyone has his own point of view'. After a year or two they advance to relativism, recognizing that different points of view have different starting points. In Perry's *Scheme* students ideally end with Commitment, accepting one framework out of many, within which one then finds a basis for choices of right and wrong, true and false. But Carol seems to be in the first stage, where she sees knowledge as a tangible thing that one can go out and get.

John's view of higher education is opposed to this, and it frustrates Carol as when he denigrates testing: 'They are not a test of your worth. They are a test of your ability to retain and spout back misinformation. Of *course* you fail them. They're *nonsense*' (23). But rather than making her at ease, this attitude enrages her. And she is completely baffled by his view of the educational process, which is not to dispense useful information:

CAROL: To provoke me?
JOHN: That's right.
CAROL: To make me mad is your job?

JOHN: That's right. To force you . . .
CAROL: . . . to make me mad is your job?
JOHN: To force you to . . . (32)

Though John never finishes this thought, it is evident where he is going is 'To force you to . . .' *think for yourself*. To Carol that is a totally alien process because she is in Perry's first position without multiplicity, looking only for the right answers. She writes everything in her notebook, and though John begs her to speak in her own words, she continually consults the written record because 'I want to make sure I have it right' (27).

These two views of education, teaching right answers versus teaching to think for oneself, to choose one right answer from among many, is one of the underlying issues of the play. It is linked by John to the similarly postmodern view that people have no fixed identity, but rather enact a self-image which can be imposed from without. John argues that he thought of himself as stupid, and so acted stupidly, when everyone told him as a child that he was stupid: 'If the young child is told he cannot understand. Then he takes it as a description of himself. What am I? *I am that which can not understand*' (16). Once he began to succeed, however, he escaped that sense of self, and began to be more successful because his new self-image was of a successful student. Again, as with the quest for right answers, the sense of a stable fixed identity is completely dismissed by postmodern sensibilities. People change dependent on circumstances and self-image, and have no fixed core or identity.

All of these issues are made manifest in *Oleanna*, and by understanding the postmodern framework of America in the 1990s, the conflicts between John and Carol become more clear. And at the same time, *Oleanna* gives focus to those social and cultural conflicts of the time in which it was written. That it continues to speak to us, and to provoke extended discussion wherever it is performed, demonstrates that those conflicts have yet to be resolved.

2 Analysis and Commentary

This chapter is a study of *Oleanna* both as a dramatic text and as a performed play that has excited comment and provoked analysis. Although plot summaries are often seen as simplistic, they are useful in sketching out the action of the play, before undertaking a broader analysis of its characters, influences, images, themes and key scenes.

Plot summary

'The play takes place in John's office' (facing page 1). The professor, John, is on the telephone discussing the purchase of a house with his wife. His student, Carol, waits patiently – she is there to discuss her grade. She is failing his course and has difficulty understanding why – she does all the work, but is getting failing grades. John explains that he is buying a house, expecting tenure from the University, and turns to her paper. He contends that she can't learn because she's 'angry', and explains he must leave for an appointment.

Carol says he thinks she is stupid, and he says he would never say that. He explains that he felt he was stupid when he was young – everyone told him he was stupid and he accepted that definition of him. He urges her to escape such a negative self-image. As he becomes 'personal', telling of his childhood, the phone rings with more problems about the house from the lawyer, Jerry. After the call, Carol asks him about his problems and he explains how he came to teaching, and how he disdains those on the Tenure Committee. He says, 'I'll make you a deal. You stay here. We'll start the whole course over. [. . .] Your grade is an "A"' (25). She objects that it is against the rules, but he says they can break the rules: 'There's nobody here but you and me' (27).

In the third part of Act One, Carol asks about his contention that education is 'hazing', and that the need to attend 'college is a prejudice.' She becomes incensed with this view, contending 'I DON'T UNDERSTAND. DO YOU SEE???' (36). She becomes overwrought, and he attempts to console her. She begins to confess her problem, 'I'm bad' and he puts his arm around her, but she spins away. Before she can explain, John's wife calls again about the house. Then the lawyer gets on the phone and finally admits the issues about the house were all a ruse to lure John there for a surprise party. John quickly packs and leaves.

Act Two opens in the same room with a three-page speech by John explaining to Carol his view of teaching and tenure and purchase of the house. She asks, 'What do you want of me' (45) and after some delay John finally asks, 'What have I done to you?' (46). She says what he has done is contained in the report to the Tenure Committee which he then reads. It contends he is 'sexist' and 'elitist' and consists mainly of quotations from John in the first act: 'He said he "liked" me. That he "liked being with me". [. . .] He told me he had problems with his wife; and that he wanted to take off the artificial stricture of Teacher and Student. He put his arm around me . . .' (48). John thinks the issue is not power but is about her feelings of anger.

Carol contends that '*hardworking students*' sacrifice to come to the school to be told they do not belong in higher education which is mere 'hazing'. She is incensed: 'That you are vile. And that you are exploitative' (52). The scene reverses as John explains that some speech is simply convention, and that human beings are not perfect. Carol seems flustered, and it seems he is winning her over until the phone rings again and he explains to the caller that the sale of the house will go through, that he will get tenure after all, because 'I'm dealing with the complaint' (55). When he hangs up, Carol realizes he is simply trying to divert her, and so she says that they should leave it to the 'conventional process' of a hearing. As she starts to leave, '*he restrains her from leaving*' and she yells for help (57).

The third act is again set in his office. John has not been home for two days thinking about his situation. He asked her to come because 'I cannot help but feel you are owed an apology' (61). As he begins to discuss the 'accusations' she corrects him 'those are not accusations. They have been *proved*' (62) and the telephone again interrupts. It is John's lawyer's office calling but he puts them off. Carol will not allow the word 'alleged' either because they 'have weighed the testimony and the evidence and have *ruled*, do you see. That you are *negligent*' (64). She takes control at this point to explain why he is losing his job. His question is 'Don't you have feelings?' (65). She says it is about principles, not feelings.

When John laments the loss of his job, she offers him a deal: to accept a list of books she and her group want banned, and to sign a statement recanting his mistakes. But when John discovers his own book is on the list, he becomes incensed. The lawyer calls and John explains to him he doesn't care that he lost his job because John realizes his new purpose is to oppose these censors. But before he finishes, the lawyer tells him they may bring criminal charges against him. Carol explains according to the law what he did was battery, and possibly attempted rape. Before he can respond, his wife calls, for he has not been home in two days, and as he attempts to console her, he yells at Carol to leave. As she does she says, 'and don't call your wife "baby"' (79). John, infuriated, '*grabs her and begins to beat her*' (79). She cowers on the floor before him. When he stops himself before bringing the chair down upon her, '(*Pause. She looks at him.*) Yes. That's right' (80).

Character analysis

John seems to be a professor of Education. His research, such as can be inferred from the play, deals with the explosion of students entering American universities after World War II. John thinks many students simply attend for cultural reasons, and don't gain anything from it.

Mamet himself, in *True and False*, argues vociferously against graduate education for actors and theatre professionals who should just leave academe, create their own companies, and perform. He carries the argument further in *South of the Northeast Kingdom* in which he explains that what was most valuable to him in school was taught in shop and typing: 'Perhaps if teachers, if elders want respect, they might do something that merits it – perhaps teach the children a skill' (2002: 53). John, similarly, contends that higher education is 'something-other-than-useful' and what most people need, however, is some 'useful' skill and therefore higher education is not useful to most people. It is this view that provokes Carol to call him 'elitist', since most students are only capable of learning skills.

John is also an elitist in wishing to send his child to private school, and questioning if he should 'have to improve the City Schools at the expense of my own interest? And, is this not simply *The White Man's Burden?*' (34). He never acknowledges this implicit racism; nor does he recognize that his desire to eliminate taxation in support of public schools is also elitist and opposed to civic virtue. And his sexism is revealed in his remark about the Tenure Committee being 'good men and true' despite, as Carol observes, one of them being a woman. Unconsciously John speaks patriarchally as he describes students with the pronoun 'he', talks of treating her like his son, and says he's not Carol's 'father'. John contends that his intentions were never sexual, 'devoid of sexual content' (70). Clearly he has no recognition, even in the third act, of any culpability, or that his actions and words are open to other interpretations.

Equally he never recognizes his use of vocabulary to intimidate his student and impress her with his learning and elevated position. From the start he says, 'You paid me the compliment, or the "obeisance"' (5) [deference], and at the start of Act Two he tries the same gambit: 'I ask myself if I engaged in heterodoxy [not in agreement with accepted beliefs], I will not say "gratuitously" for I do not care to posit orthodoxy [adhering to accepted beliefs] as a given good . . .' (43). In the third act, when she has control, however, Carol does not allow him to start the discussion with words which need more precise definition: 'accusations' 'alleged' and 'indictment' being the first three she challenges.

His view of education in general is that it fails because students see themselves as failures, and the whole system is designed to make them see themselves this way: 'you have to look at how you act. And say: If that's what I did [fail], that must be how I think of myself [as a failure]' (22). For him, therefore, the key to education is how students 'feel' and that is a word he uses over and over. John assumes that Carol is 'angry' when, at least at the start of the play, she is not. But ironically he provokes her anger by continually insisting this is what she must be feeling. He sees these feelings as blockages to education. So, with this view of postmodern subjectivity and fluid identity, one would think he would recognize his predicament. After all he realizes 'We can only interpret the behavior of other through the screen we [. . .] Through the screen we create' (19–20). Yet, ironically, he does not apply his own insight to his situation: 'I didn't understand. Then I thought: is it not always at those points at which we reckon ourselves unassailable that we are most vulnerable and . . . ' (45). At the end of the play, however, John does turn into the very monster which Carol accused him of being when he calls her a 'cunt' and beats her up – exerting male strength to dominate and force her into subservience.

The characters have no last names, no ethnicity, no geography, virtually no background. About John we know nothing other than he was told he was stupid and he came to teaching late in life. He has a wife, Grace, and 'the boy'. Carol, by contrast, says she comes 'from a different *social* [. . .] a different economic' (8) background, one assumes. But nothing about her speech or behaviour marks her as any different from any other middle class student. Unlike John, She is not at all postmodern. Like a strict fundamentalist, she insists on a clear contrast between 'right' and 'wrong' even at the end of the play: 'You're wrong. I'm not wrong. You're wrong' (68). From the beginning, when she shows such reliance on her notes, and desires to get it all down correctly: 'I want to make sure that I have it right. [. . .] I want to know everything that went on' (28). This last line is a through-line for her, a desire 'to know everything' is excessive, but she is determined.

Carol poses a problem for both actors and audiences. She seems incompetent in the first act, having few lines except to object that she doesn't understand John. Then, in Acts Two and Three, she becomes increasingly strong and dominant, a figure of power, teaching the teacher. How can one explain the reversal?

Her behaviour seems to confirm John's theory – when she thinks of herself as stupid, she is stupid; when she gains confidence and thinks of herself as smart, she is smart. Many readers, however, think that the 'group' to which she alludes must have made her into someone quite different – a strong, powerful feminist.

In Mamet's view, this 'is a tragedy about power' (Norman, 1995: 125); 'each [character]'s point of view is correct' (125). That is 'the points she makes about power and privilege – I believe them all' (125), Mamet says in the same interview. But as Carol grows in power and strength, she becomes as much of a tyrant as John is when he is the patriarchal one in power in the first act. By the end of the play, when she is intervening to take control of John's personal life, telling him how to address his wife, she is carried away by her sense of power, just as he had been in Act One.

Influences, genre and style

Mamet's plays are a fusion of conventional realism with the theatre of the absurd. The realism is reflected in the social problem *Oleanna* addresses. Unlike the realist, however, Mamet refuses to point towards a solution. One absurdist influence is Nobel Prize winning British dramatist Harold Pinter, who directed the first London production of *Oleanna*. Ruby Cohn (1995) has done the most extended comparison and contrast of their work in *Anglo–American Interplay in Recent Drama*. In addition, others have pointed to parallels with absurdist Ionesco's *The Lesson* in which the male professor kills his female student. James McDermott (2006) cites Beckett's *Endgame* as a source of 'the stark language of Mamet's mature dramas,' though Mamet retains realism's 'concrete desire and intentionality' as well as 'a bare minimum of "story"' (134).

Assessing Pinter's influence on Mamet is difficult because it is so pervasive. From the time Mamet was 'a kid' Pinter 'was always a, a hero of mine and really was responsible to a large extent for me starting to write. And then he was very, very helpful and, and generous to me – and still is – at many points in my career, in promoting my work and directing my work' (Rose, 1994: 173–4). The specific influence is in language and ways of constructing experience: 'You spoke of demotic language. That's what he was writing in all the *Revue Sketches* and *A Night Out* and *The Birthday Party*. And all of those plays dramatized things that I'd heard and seen and experienced. And they didn't appear to be a traditional dramatic expression. They were thrilling' (Isaacs, 1998: 219).

At the Second International David Mamet Conference in London, Jack Shepherd, the original Ricky Roma in *Glengarry Glen Ross*, gave a simple illustration of the difference between Pinter pauses and Mamet's. Pinter's starting point is that whoever speaks loses in a struggle for dominance. Dominant characters, when forced to speak, simply rattle off jargon, a kind of demotic language, filling space without giving anything away. But the loser is revealed in the '(*Pause*)' stage direction. These characters simply run out of things to say, can no longer fill the void. The other person refuses to help out by breaking the silence. Mamet's characters, by contrast, are thinking so quickly, especially in *Oleanna*, that the ellipses that come between phrases actually indicate that their minds are working so fast and furiously that they can't come up with words quickly enough. In both cases, however, the audience fills in the gaps since the characters cannot. Missing parts are an important technique for both playwrights. Aston is missing brain-parts/ memory in Pinter's *The Caretaker* that simply can't be filled in. In *Oleanna*, crucial scenes which would indicate who is 'right' are missing – John in class, John with other female students, John and Carol at the Tenure Committee hearing. Debra Eisenstadt, Carol in the film, told me that Mamet actually wrote classroom scenes but they were not used in the film. By cutting these pieces out, the work forces the audience to fill in the gaps.

Verna Foster explains the parallel with Ionesco's *The Lesson*: 'In both plays the power inherent in the professor's role as controller and purveyor of knowledge (represented in part by his authority over the meaning of words) is ultimately expressed as sexual power over the student' (1995: 37). What is different, however, is that Mamet's play goes in the same direction, but then reverses the power, so that the student is in control after the first act. In this way he carries the audience out of a familiar situation, a teacher's power over his student, like Ionesco's, into an uncharted territory. In Mamet's play, as a result, the audience is deprived of its usual assurance, and either will fall into old models of thought, or recognize the exploration as a new experience or suffer with the ambiguity.

Realism's heritage is evident in the parallels with Lillian Hellman's *The Children's Hour* (1934). Both her play and *Oleanna* deal with difficult-to-verify sexual accusations, and both were consequently banned or protested when first staged. Both are set in schools, but the line between home and school is blurred; both deal with female students, and accusations against teachers; and both deal with sexual accusations which by definition are murky and matters of perception. Yet both employ the conventions of realism which normally require that the hidden secrets be revealed by the end of the play.

The difference between them is that we know from the outset that the girl in The *Children's Hour* is lying in her accusations. Karen is certainly not a lesbian. But her colleague Martha wonders if, subconsciously, she might have had lesbian desires for Karen and out of guilt kills herself. The play never resolves the issue of Martha's desires. But the audience knows the truth of the situation, that Mary lied about them, and this is finally revealed. In William Worthen's view, this is how realism works to reassure an audience that it can read beneath the surface, see into people's private affairs, and know the secrets (17). Mamet rejects that assumption, leading the audience to expect that such a revelation is coming, but we never learn why Carol thinks she's 'bad' or the secret that she has never told another person.

Rather, the audience is left to face its own failure to read the situation. That was my experience in viewing Mamet's production when he moved it to Washington. Since I had heard of the controversies caused in New York, I looked forward to this production. I was stunned at the end of the first act when the lights came up – and I thought the act was a waste! Where was the sexual harassment? Why spend an act introducing the characters without raising the central issue of the play. How easily duped I was. I really fell for Mamet's trick, and so the second act completely devastated me. I realized that I was as blind as John – and came to see the whole first act entirely from Carol's perspective.

Thereafter I saw my relationship to my own students in a wholly new light, and had to examine my methods to try to reverse many hidden and unconscious assumptions. For I had myself written 'What could this mean' without seeing how someone like Carol might interpret that question. I think the play is uniquely tragic in that the experience of tragic recognition happens to the audience members outside the play, rather than to John in the play.

In many interviews Mamet contends that *Oleanna* is an Aristotelian tragedy (David Mamet in *Conversation*, 2001: 118–19; 124–5; 144–5). Mamet believes that John comes to a classic tragic recognition and reversal at the end of the play. His career is now ruined, and John loses his whole comfortable identity as professor which he had at the beginning. Calling Carol a 'cunt' and beating her seems to reveal him to be the sexist, patriarchal antifeminist that Carol contends he is. And yet the words do not support this as his recognition. He only says, after beating her and stopping himself with the chair raised above her, '. . . well . . .' and she responds twice, 'Yes. That's right' (80). This certainly constitutes a reversal, but the recognition seems incomplete.

In fact, John never acknowledges that he is at fault in any way. Even if he has no intention of sexually harassing Carol, he must see that what he says and does is open to misinterpretation. At the end of the play, grand inquisitor Carol demands that he accept that he is not the one allowed to interpret his actions as 'devoid of sexual content' (70).

> CAROL: Do you hold yourself harmless from the charge of sexual exploitativeness . . .?
> JOHN: Well, I . . . I . . . I . . . (71)

And of course, Carol never comes close to recognizing her own tragedy – that of being swept away by power. She is always sure she is right, with no ambiguity.

As a result, there is no real recognition, though there is clearly a reversal. John recognizes that he has finally destroyed his job and security, lost the house, beaten a student and is criminally guilty without doubt. But the reason he beats her is essentially that he blames her for his downfall, rather than seeing or accepting any fault in himself. Without that recognition, it does not appear to be a fully tragic experience.

Mamet's concept of tragedy is not entirely Aristotelian – it is more basically Freudian. He explains: 'But that tragedy is about horrific things. It's about bringing the hidden to light so that one can grieve. And that's why tragedy, in the perfect form, is cleansing, because it enables us to deal with repression. It enables us to take the repressed and investigate it. And, as Freud would have said, instead of living a happy life, be more capable to live a life of ordinary misery' (Shulgasser, 1998: 209). In this view, it is not the character whose repression is unearthed, but the audience's. This correlates with Mamet's contention that the playwright exposes the 'National Dream-Life', the collective repressed. *Oleanna* does this with sexism and patriarchal privilege, as well as revealing how power corrupts whoever holds it.

The Jesuit President of my College, Father Greg Lucey, attending my production of Mamet's earlier *Sexual Perversity in Chicago* – seeing students crammed in to every nook and cranny of the theatre, observed – 'this experience was really cathartic for this campus.' That is, the sexist Bernie Litko was unearthed – but only to be held up for examination, to be seen rather than repressed, and so to be exorcized in true Jesuit tradition. *Oleanna* performs a similar function. After my production, the audience stayed for an hour discussing the play. What most excited me was that faculty and students, African American students and whites, Asians and Hispanics, male and female, all felt empowered to speak, and to speak as equals. It was a unique experience because the play not only encouraged so many different perspectives, and gave each speaker a voice.

In postmodern theory, individual fates are not the focus as they were for the Enlightenment tradition that culminated in realism and the modernist experiment. Rather Althusser argues the problem is that everyone is brainwashed by commonly accepted ideology. As a result, the villain of the play is essentially the system itself which Mamet attacks – an academic utopia which first empowers the (male) professor to lord it over female students, and then endows the female students with power over the male professors. And in both cases, the empowered are totally unaware of how the change in circumstance changes them. John's theory that people are affected by how others view them (as failures) dominates the first act. But neither he nor Carol ever recognizes how they themselves are subject to the same blindness when they gain power.

The title of the play, *Oleanna,* refers to a Norwegian folksong about creating a utopia. While academe may construe itself as a utopia, in Mamet's play it is dystopic. And it is not the characters' fault that the tragedy ensues. Mamet argues rather the fault is in the world they inhabit:

> This play – and the film – is a tragedy about power. These are two people with a lot to say to each other; with legitimate affection for each other. But protecting their positions becomes more important than pursuing their own best interests. And that leads them down the slippery slope to a point where, at the end of the play, they tear each other's throat out. [. . .] the points she makes about power and privilege – I believe them all. If I didn't believe them, the play wouldn't work as well. It is a play about two people, and each person's point of view is correct. And yet they wind up destroying each other. (Norman, 1995: 125)

What is clear from the passage is that the destruction is not the fault of one or the other, as it would be in a conventional tragedy. The fault is endemic to the system which empowers them into 'protecting their own positions'.

Close reading of key scenes

Mamet is very precise in his dramatic construction. Despite the indirection of the characters, there is an exact structure to each act.

Act One

In Act One, there are four main movements. In the first, John tells Carol that she is failing, and attempts to leave as this is not a scheduled appointment (1–13). The second occurs when she says that he is telling her she is stupid, and he drops everything to tell her that he too was treated as stupid early in his life, and was scarred by it (13–28). In the third movement (28–36), he explains his theory of higher education and she becomes increasingly outraged and offended by his view that not everyone should go to university. In the fourth movement, Carol explodes over her failure to understand, breaks down and is consoled by him until the final phone call (36–41).

To understand Mamet's dramaturgy one must recognize that it is very difficult, if not impossible, for his characters to say what they mean, or to come to the point. Part of the reason for this is that they have so much going on in their heads that they can't limit their thoughts to one set of words. Another reason is that they want to get something from the other person, and most often use indirection as the strategy to manipulate the other into giving them, or at least not to be refused, because of a direct approach.

Thus the opening of each act does not start, as old style drama might, with someone saying what he or she wants, or is interested in, but rather the opposite – with indirection. Carol comes to John's office to see what she can do to improve her grade in his course. But does she say that? No, not until two-thirds of the way through the act does she blurt out, 'I want to know about my grade' (24). So how does she start? She cannot think what to ask, how to open, and first there is a Pause. Then she finally blurts out, instead, 'What is a term of art?' He's surprised, not sure she really said that, (*Pause*) 'I'm sorry . . .?' (2). And again, she tries to think of a way to back out of this, but cannot find one: (*Pause*) 'What is a "term of art"?' His response is logical, 'Is that what you want to talk about?' (3). Already things have gotten off on the wrong foot, and they will never recover.

Carol's opening line 'What is a term of art?' foreshadows the language theme of the play. It reflects the postmodern view that words do not denote precise things in the outer world, but rather are dependent on context for meaning. Technically, as John explains it, a term of art is a legal concept: 'It seems to mean a term, which has come, through its use, to mean something more specific than the words would, to someone not acquainted with them . . . indicate' (3). That is, it refers to words which mean something more specific because of use (context) which is not as broad as the dictionary definition of the word.

Carol's lack of understanding in the first act is pointedly displayed whenever John refers to 'theory' (24) or 'concept' or 'let's see if we can wring some worth from the statistics. Eh?' (35). Each time she reacts strongly, cutting him off to say she does not understand. All the references, of course, are to words which require interpretations, which are not simply facts, but are theories, and require more than rote learning. Carol is too factually based to be able to deal with them, and each time John raises one of these issues, she reacts as if to an electric shock.

The problem with John's theory is that it deals with the whole idea of seeing truth from a variety of perspectives, a concept which completely confuses Carol. Their conflicts reflect Perry's developmental psychology in *Forms of Intellectual and Moral Development in the College Years*. Like Perry's college student at the initial stage of intellectual development, Carol is a dualist, seeing answers as either right or wrong, and similarly all moral issues as good or bad. This kind of dualistic student, according to Perry, thinks the teacher has all the right answers, and the student's job is simply to get them, write them down, and memorize them. John tries to assuage her, but she just gets more upset. What frustrates her is clear from the passage on page 12. She sees knowledge, 'something they didn't *know*' as an object, something one can go out and 'get'. The teacher's job is simply to '*help*' the student to get it. When this approach to learning fails, she blames herself saying over and over, 'I don't *understand*.' All of these are words Mamet italicizes for emphasis.

John attempts to help (also repeated three times) her by trying to show her that learning has more to do with frameworks of understanding, rather than with the knowledge itself as a possession. This corresponds to Perry's middle levels, where there seem to be a multiplicity of frameworks, rather than a single one with a single right answer. To explain this John tells about how he was thought to be stupid as well: '[. . .] my earliest, and most persistent memories are of being told that I was stupid. 'You have such *intelligence*. Why must you behave so stupidly?' (16). Like her, John plays off the idea of some 'people' who get knowledge, and who understand, against his view of himself as someone less than a complete person, inadequate. And he wants Carol to see that she is making the same dualistic dichotomy, resulting in seeing herself as a failure.

Entering into this framework, according to John, is what makes her into a failure, or at least did for him: 'If you are told . . . Listen to this. If the young child is told he cannot understand. Then he takes it as a description of himself. What am I? I am *that which can not understand*' (16–17). This exchange is a perfect microcosm of the whole conflict of the first act of the play. John is not trying to teach facts, but to teach frameworks. And the framework he is trying to give Carol is a new attitude towards knowledge which is that it is not based on the traditional rote methods: 'learn, study, retain'. Instead, his view of education has to do with teaching students self-esteem, rather than berating them for failures which lead to anger and frustration. From his perspective, it is the view of themselves as failures which makes it impossible for them to learn, not a deficiency of intellect.

But Carol cannot yet grasp this, even though she is living proof of the point. She is still looking for some tangible knowledge that she can hold on to, rather than an attitude towards learning, towards herself as a person, and towards her students when she becomes a teacher. The reason that John refers to the traditional content of education as '*garbage*' and '*nonsense*' (which she later rejects on page 23) is because it is not the content, but the way in which the learning is presented that is most important. Because, in his experience, even though he was 'intelligent', he was treated as being stupid, and as a result he thought of himself this way and could not learn.

This idea of self-image is taken even further as John extends the consequence by showing that this view of oneself then is carried over into guilt, and self-laceration and self-destruction. He tells a story: 'The pilot is flying the plane. He thinks: Oh, my God, my mind's been drifting! Oh, my *God*! What kind of a cursed imbecile am I' (18), and crashes the plane because he was not thinking clearly. The point of the story is that this view of blaming oneself is entirely a matter of self-image, and of the framework in which the pilot chooses to view his mistake. The lesson Carol should learn is that she is defeating herself, expecting to fail as soon as she has some difficulty grasping a concept. That was John's experience: 'And you will say: "I am incapable of . . . " and everything in you will think these two things. "I must. But I can't"' (19). John's point is that this kind of ultimate test anxiety will lead directly to failure. And more importantly, it is not even the reality of a test, but any situation which she perceives as a test will immediately trigger all of the negative and self-destructive moves that are latent in her mind.

In the second act John suffers exactly the fate he imagines in the first. Like the pilot in his own story, or the student who faces a test, John becomes self-lacerating and then finally self-destructive. The key point, however, is that this is self-destruction – not Carol's fault but his own, when he flips from one framework, the positive one in which he is in control, to the negative one in which he sees himself as a failure.

John acknowledges this fear beneath the surface as he tries to explain once more his personal discovery of these two frameworks:

> I came late to teaching. And I found it Artificial. The notion of 'I know and you do not'; and I saw an *exploitation* in the education process. [. . .] I hated everyone who was in a position of a 'boss' because I knew I was going to fail. Because I was a fuckup. I was just no goddamned good. When I . . . late in life . . . (*Pause*). (22)

John's anti-authoritarian hatred becomes clear in this passage. And it is also what he unleashes, inadvertently, in the second act when he begins to see himself back in the position of being tested – for it is that situation which triggers his suppressed self-hatred, which he takes out on the rest of the world.

That this will be his fate seems evident as he describes his test-taking bias, and merges that with the view of the Tenure Committee as the ultimate testing authority:

> The Tenure Committee. Come to judge me. The Bad Tenure Committee. The 'Test'. Do you see? They put me to the test. Why, they had people voting on me I wouldn't employ to wax my car. And yet, I go before The Great Tenure Committee, and I have an urge, to *vomit*, to, to, to puke my *badness* on the table, to show them: 'I'm no good. Why would you pick *me*?' (23)

In this speech John very quickly dissolves from the teacher of considerable ego, seeing others as 'idiots', to the complete reverse with a desire to display all his '*badness*' before The Great Tenure Committee. While this demonstrates John's own instability, it also proves his point: the different frameworks, the different ways of looking at knowledge, produce completely different responses inside of the learner himself, one positive, one negative. But tests seem to assume objective knowledge and an objective learner, rather than one who is subject to feelings of inadequacy and for that reason fails.

There is no objective reality such as Carol appears to envision in John's world of higher education. This becomes clear in the second act when Carol as well seems to undergo a complete transformation. Some critics are upset about this, as seemingly unmotivated, but a key point of the play is that the way one perceives a thing radically changes depending on one's internal orientation to it. From this perspective, Carol's 'group', which alarms so many critics, has simply given her self-confidence and a different orientation towards John. Instead of thinking she will fail, she sees herself as in the right, and she does not fail. Rather, John fails as he begins to put the whole action into the context of a 'test' at which, as with the Tenure Committee, he will not only fail, but self-destruct. So, ironically, his point about educational frameworks is proven by her reversal, as well as by his own.

But Carol cannot understand either the idea that truth is a matter of the framework from which one looks, nor the idea that self-image determines outcome. For her, the external is objective and real. And since she cannot understand John, 'I don't know what you're *saying*', Carol seems to fill in a context which she does understand, a sexual one, and then uses that as her way to interpret the encounter. Thus she finds a more specific meaning to the words than they might otherwise mean ['a term of art'], based on the context of being in a closed-door office with an older, male professor. And lots of his words are open to such an implied sexual invitation:

> JOHN: No, let's get on with it. (5)
> JOHN: I'm talking to you the way I wish that someone had talked to me. I don't know how to do it other than to be personal.
> CAROL: Why would you want to be personal with me? (19)

CAROL: Why did you stay here with me? [. . .] When you should have gone.
JOHN: Because I like you.
CAROL: You like me. (20–1)
JOHN: If we're going to take off the artificial stricture of 'Teacher' and 'Student,' why should my problems be any more a mystery than your own? Of course I have problems. As you saw. [. . .] with my wife . . . with work. (21–2)
JOHN: Your grade for the whole term is an 'A.' If you will come back and meet with me. A few more times. Your grade's an 'A.' (25)
CAROL: There are rules.
JOHN: Well. We'll break them.
CAROL: How can we?
JOHN: We won't tell anybody.
CAROL: Is that all right?
JOHN: I say that's fine. (26)

Clearly this set of quotations is liable, taken as a group, to imply a sexual subtext. Like 'a term of art', words can be given a specific context which is not as broad as the dictionary definitions, and Carol supplies such a context to give all these words a sexual meaning. No doubt John does not intend them this way. And no doubt this is how Carol, baffled by his language and his 'concepts', understands him. In her desperation, she assumes he is sexually propositioning her by supplying an old stereotype to the encounter, viewing it in her default context of sexuality:

CAROL: Why would you do this for me?
JOHN: I like you. Is that so difficult for you to . . .
CAROL: Um . . .
JOHN: There's no one here but you and me. (*Pause*)
CAROL: All right. I did not understand. When you referred . . . (27)

For Carol the recognition of sexual innuendo seems to coalesce with this second 'I like you', and she quickly tries to change back to the subject matter of the course. Clearly, in so thinking, I have entered into the text to give my own understanding of the character's motive. But the point of the play, and this cannot be insisted upon enough, is that this is what we do – as an audience – we put ourselves into the situation, and the result is not an objective assessment but rather one so subjective as to make the play a Rorschach test to reveal our own individual assumptions and unconscious ways of understanding.

The crucial moment in Carol's performance is the end of the first act. What is she about to confess when John gets the call and leaves? She is trembling on the brink of a revelation:

> CAROL: I can't talk about this.
> JOHN: It's all right. Tell me.
> CAROL: Why do you want to know this?
> JOHN: I don't want to know. I want to know whatever you . . .
> CAROL: I always . . .
> JOHN: . . . good . . .
> CAROL: I always . . . all my life . . . I have never told anyone this . . . (38)

Carol's confession is expressed almost entirely in negatives: 'I can't' (three times); 'I didn't' (three times); 'never', 'not'; and the direct statements: 'I feel bad [. . .] I'm bad.' But since there is no positive assertion, her secret remains hidden. As soon as she begins, 'All my life . . .' she is cut off by the telephone call and John leaves her hanging. When Act Two opens, she has brought her complaint to the Tenure Committee, and that issue consumes the last two acts.

This confessional scene differs markedly from the more complete realist's version. It has the familiar postmodern markers: it is fragmented, continually interrupted, and ultimately aborted. This much one might expect in postmodernism. If understood through realistic conventions, the audience is given continual hints here of some dark secret that Carol has hidden inside. But unlike the realist writer's confession the audience never learns the secret in the character's heart, and in this case no allusion is ever made back to this secret. Thus the author is no longer the authority who predetermines interpretation. In this open-ended situation, there is no evidence that Mamet had anything more in mind to explain Carol's secret. Actor, Audience and Author are all left with only the text, and no subtext to interpret.

And yet this aborted confession is central to the meaning and experience of the play. It certainly was for me when I saw Mamet's production at the Kennedy Center with Eisenstadt and Macy – I thought John had led Carol on shamelessly to reveal her innermost secret, and then, as she started to confess, he just abandoned her and left for his party. As I saw the performance, it was not quite sexual abuse, but it was certainly some form of student abuse. What is important is not *what* her secret was, but John's total lack of recognition of her vulnerability at that moment.

In the play, Mamet evades revealing Carol's secret when the final telephone interruption of the Act informs us that all of the frustrating calls were a ruse to get John to the surprise party. The trick has also been played on the audience – 'there are those who would say it's a form of aggression . . . A surprise' (41).

Act Two

The requirement in reading, acting or directing a script is to grant the writer what Henry James calls 'the donné', the given situation. But when a character deviates from the expected path, it is crucial to examine what causes the deviation. In Act Two John begins with a long rambling monologue about how he came to teaching. Since he does not come to the point, Carol must ask him, once he takes a breath after three pages, 'What is it you want of me?' (45). But he takes off again, moving by indirection around what he wants, noting that 'I was hurt' first, and then 'Finally, I did not understand.' But he still can't come to the point, and takes off on another ramble. At last he concludes:

> I asked you here to . . . in the spirit of *investigation*, to ask you
> . . . to ask . . . (*Pause*) What have I done to you? (*Pause*) (46)

Notice that the lead-in to his real question is still marred by continual starts and stops. And when she says nothing in response to his question as with Pinter, he follows it up, filling in the silence, trying to amplify: 'And, and, I suppose, how I can make amends. Can we not settle this now? It's pointless, really, and I want to know' (46). Since Carol never answers what he's done to her, he is forced to continue – to ask how he can atone. He doesn't say he's sorry, nor does he quite offer to 'make amends'. He just wants to know what price she'll ask.

When Carol rejects this as an attempt to 'force me to retract' he seems to be off on another lecture/digression about 'The Stoical Philosophers' but he quickly notices her reaction and stops himself: 'Now: Think: I know that you're upset. Just tell me Literally. Literally: What wrong have I done you' (47). So he repeats the key question. This brings us to the centre of the second act. She's brought charges, as yet we don't know what they are – but we know he is hurt and upset by her having brought them. Again his formulation is exceedingly strange – three words out of twelve followed by colons – Two words in a row?

All of this is designed to tell the actor about the character and how to deliver the lines. What is the actor supposed to do to convey the punctuation of a double colon? 'Now: Think:' Certainly there must be pauses between each word; it is less of a full stop than the full period that Carol is given 3 pages later: 'You. Do. Not. Have. The. Power' (50). But something else must be going on or Mamet could have used his and Pinter's favourite stage direction: '(*Pause*)'. The point is simply that one must stop and analyse when a shift like this happens from the usual way that the author writes. Actor and director must talk it over, try out different deliveries, to try to find a suitable means of expression.

This is all the more true when Carol replies to John, and for the first time, at least in this act, she does not express herself directly, but takes up his strategy of indirection, of backing away from her first formulation before finishing it. And since this comes at the crucial moment of answering what he's 'done to' her, it is a telling slip:

> Whatever you have done to me – to the extent that you've done it to me, do you know, rather than to me as a student, and, so, to the student body, is contained in my report. (47)

The line is crucial for actor and director, because clearly Carol is being evasive. Why? Why won't she answer his direct question, especially when it is asked for the second time, and when it is a crucial and central issue. She starts indirectly – then backs away even from asserting that it is she who is his victim, and instead expands her charges to include the whole student body. Why can't she just say, 'you harassed me sexually by asking me to come to your office, see you in private, because you are having trouble with your wife, and offered me an A as an inducement?'

And another question is why she is so reluctant to speak. For Carol everything must be written down. Why? She reads from her notes of what he says, and her charges are all reflections of what he said, which she must have transcribed as she sat in his office in the first act. But rather than telling him what he's done wrong, she tells him to 'Consult the Report'. Because, she insists, those are her words. But why couldn't she tell him what he did to her?

In the report is the list of remarks he made which clearly imply sexual harassment. They all lead to the implication of grade change for sex. But after Carol and John discuss these charges, which he denigrates as 'pointless' (46) and 'ludicrous' (48), she virtually starts the meeting over: 'Professor. I came here as a favor' (50). When she tells him what has her most upset, however, it is not sex that is the issue, but a combination of his personal style and the approach he takes to the subject matter of the course, higher education:

> What gives you the right. Yes. To speak to a woman in your private . . . Yes. Yes. I'm sorry. I'm sorry. You feel yourself empowered . . . you say to yourself. To strut. To posture. To 'perform.' To 'Call me in here . . .' Eh? You say that higher education is a joke. And treat it as such, you treat it as such. And confess to a taste to play the Patriarch in your class. To grant this. To deny that. To embrace your students. (51)

There is a clear confusion here between sexual abuse and the abuse of power. Being a 'Patriarch' is constructed as doubleness. The issue of power is mixed together with his view of higher education and his way of treating students, granting or denying them whatever. She puts the treatment of 'a woman' in juxtaposition with his 'performance' and those together with his view of 'higher education'.

After this she has a full-page speech explaining what he has done to her, but it is not sexual in nature – 'You confess. You love the Power. To deviate. To invent, to transgress . . . to transgress whatever norms have been established for us. And you think it's charming to "question" in yourself this taste to mock and destroy. But you should question it. Professor' (52). Her appeal in this speech is that the students who sacrificed so much to attend the institution are being told their sacrifices are not worthwhile by the faculty member himself. And she sees this as a pose and hypocrisy because he is teaching at this very institution he denigrates.

It almost makes one wonder if she is doing a bait and switch, for the charges aren't the same as those which she really resents. Of course, the sexual charges are clear offences. But teaching 'transgression' is not quite so easy to use as grounds for denying tenure. So she seems to have used the charges that would make her case, and doesn't quite notice that her deepest resentments aren't the charges that she's written in her report to the Tenure Committee. What is curious is that her charges, subsequently, alternate between anger at his teachings, which she finds insulting to her aspirations, and accusations about sexual harassment. What she wrote to the Committee, lines taken out of context, make perfect sense in sequence – and clearly indicate sexual misconduct. But her charges seem to wobble back and forth between elitism and sexism. Elitism is not a firing offence; sexism usually is. And Carol makes the charges that will stick.

From the outset, her failure to answer 'What have I done to you' leaves him at a loss so he finally blunders further – 'and what can I do to make it up to you'. The first and most interesting thing about his question is that it jumps over a number of steps. He does not offer any form of apology. He does not offer any form of denial over the sexual charges. Instead, he assumes that the issue is one of feelings, not of substance, and that what charges she has brought are of no import, but simply represent a little girl's hurt feelings. And of course he sees nothing insulting about this. But she is insulted, and asks if his purpose is really simply to get her to retract her charges.

John says that he understands her, that she is angry. But is she? This was his view in the first act, and he kept asserting it over and over – it is clearly part of his theory of education – that students may be blocked from learning when they are angry. But it is hardly a universal solution, as he seems to employ it. And he insists on it so often in the first act that he finally makes her angry: 'Yes. I understand. I understand. You're *hurt*. You're *angry*. Yes. I think your anger is betraying you. Down a path which helps no one' (50). Tragically he creates the situation he predicts; she does the same later in charging him with sexism, until he finally beats her at the end of the play using a sexist epithet. He becomes the male chauvinist pig she accuses him of being – but was he really that before, or did she goad him into becoming one? Did he goad her into becoming 'a "deranged" What? revolutionary?' (53) Did he create the anger within her? Once he reads the charges he concludes they are '*ludicrous*' inciting her to anger if she hadn't had it before.

After her rants against him as 'vile, exploitative' as she packs up to go, he stops her with 'Nice day, isn't it?' And his explanation to her of conventional conversation, has a surprising effect. She is suddenly left without words, unable to respond:

> CAROL: . . . wait . . .
> JOHN: Yes. I want to hear it.
> CAROL: . . . the . . .
> JOHN: Yes. Tell me frankly.
> CAROL: . . . my position . . .
> JOHN: I want to hear it. In your own words. What you want. And what you feel.
> CAROL: . . . I . . .
> JOHN: . . . yes . . .
> CAROL: My Group.
> JOHN: Your 'Group' . . .? *(Pause)* (54)

John's explanation of convention nearly involves admitting imperfection, 'flawed as I may be'. He derails Carol with his calm and rational argument, diverting her from her complaints against him.

But just when he seems to be on the brink of winning her over, the phone rings and as he tries to get rid of the caller, presumably Jerry, he starts by trying to head him off: 'Then tell her I think it's going to be fine. *(Pause)* [. . .] Just *trust* me. Be . . . well, I'm dealing with the complaint' (55). As she overhears this conversation, with his sense that he is 'dealing with' her complaint, she picks up his words: 'No. I think we should stick to the process [. . .] the conventional process as you said' (56). At this point, as she tries to leave, he restrains her, and she yells for help. He is lost as he is on the brink of getting her to withdraw her complaint. His holding her at the end of the act is simply an indication of his desperation – he almost won her over, only to have the telephone interrupt and as a result lose his verbal hold on her.

Act Three

Oleanna clearly raises the issue of empty signifiers. The first act, in performance at least, gave me no hint of sexual harassment. But by the end of the play I was convinced not only of John's abuse of Carol, but of my own blindness to words and gestures which can be interpreted in quite different ways. I saw the audience at the Kennedy Center divide itself as it voted after the performance on who was right. The ushers taking votes on a chalkboard simply illustrated the lack of any fixed reality, as some of us saw one thing, and others quite the opposite.

In such circumstances, power comes to the fore. If there is no fixed reality, if everything is a matter of interpretation, then whoever has the most power wins. John wins in *Oleanna* in the first act because he's the professor, buying a house, with a family – all the trappings of academic and middle class power. But in the second and third acts, Carol finds power of her own – through her group, the Tenure Committee, and the courts to wrest interpretative power away from John. Even when we know, as we do in *Oleanna* where we see all that happens, there is no certainty – is it sexual harassment or not? The issue is decided not by some external norms of truth, but by power – first the professor holds the power, then the student and Tenure Committee do. Whoever is aligned with the power structure is able to interpret the 'truth' of the incident. As a result, in the beginning he interprets words for her; in the last act, she does that for him.

If this were a conventional realistic play, then the buried secret of the first act would have to be revealed in the final act. But this is not that kind of play. Causality is not individual, and so Carol's feelings of being 'bad' which she's never confessed to anyone are not the issue or the motivation. Nor is her 'group' ever explained. These are not the motives. They are misdirections by magician Mamet to keep us from seeing that it is a system in which we all exist that creates the tragedy, not individual background, or support group, or other conventional kind of realistic cause.

This time it is John who is trying to get Carol to change his grade – to forgive and forget. But like Carol in the first act who thinks she did everything right, taking notes, reading his book, John thinks his good intentions towards his students, as he conceives of them, make him totally innocent. Once again, though, he fails to start out by saying what he wants, and only alienates her further by saying he called her in for her own good. Finally, he gets to the point – 'I cannot help but feel you are owed an apology (*Pause*)' (61). But he does not offer an apology. Further, the passive voice hides him – not 'I owe you an apology.' He does not think he owes her one. And he never makes one.

Carol is only there to instruct him – she wants 'understanding'. She finally beats him into submission over 'freedom of thought' which he believes in – and which she rightly notes means only his freedom – no recognition of her freedom or the Committee's to find him in error. At this point, there is a kind of levelling and misrecognitions are dropped: 'I know what you think I am. [. . .] a frightened, repressed, confused, I don't know, abandoned young thing of some doubtful sexuality, who wants, power and revenge' (68). And once this is acknowledged, she concludes: 'Do you hate me now?' and he admits he does. Carol replies that this is the first moment of honesty between them.

At this point she tries to show him that it is the power he hates, not her, and she explains what it is to be 'subject to that power' (70). To do this, she repeats that the sexist language and touching, which he says 'was devoid of sexual content' was not, in her view. Currently California state law is moving towards her position. In the past, the standard of misbehaviour was – what would an objective viewer think when witnessing the behaviour? But California has led the way in arguing that there if there is no objective viewer, then the standard instead should consider – what did the person perceive? Clearly Carol perceived sexual content and the Tenure Committee agreed with her: 'I say it was not. I SAY IT WAS NOT. Don't you begin to see . . .? Don't you begin to understand? IT'S NOT FOR YOU TO SAY' (70).

As a result he begins to back down:

> JOHN: I take your point. I see there is much good in what you refer to.
> CAROL: . . . do you think so . . .?
> JOHN: . . . but, and this is not to say that I cannot change, in those things in which I am deficient . . . But, the . . .
> CAROL: Do you hold yourself harmless from the charge of sexual exploitativeness . . .? (*Pause*)
> JOHN: We, I . . . I . . . I . . . You know I, as I said. I . . . think I am not too old to learn, and I can learn, I . . . (71)

Clearly John cannot admit to wrongdoing of any kind, and while Carol keeps trying to trap him in a corner, all he concedes is that he *can* change. But he never recognizes or accepts any wrongdoing. And he finally returns, once again, to his job. 'What's the use. It's over' (71).

John lacks a tragic recognition of what he has done wrong, though he realizes he has lost. This is magnified by Carol's total lack of recognition or reversal, making this a curious kind of tragedy. It is not exactly Aristotelian despite Mamet's belief. Aristotle's ideal was *Oedipus Rex* because Oedipus undergoes recognition and reversal.

But *Oleanna* is a different kind of tragedy, almost a tragedy of misrecognition. The paradigmatic hero of this sort is Willy Loman. For 17 years he believed Biff hated him, 'spite is the word of your undoing'. But at the very end, he realizes, finally, that Biff really loves him. 'Always has loved you, Pop' says Happy. With this realization, Willy kills himself for the $20,000 insurance money to pay back his son for loving him, rather than accepting the gift of love. In *The Bacchae* Pentheus never realizes his fault in rejecting Bacchus. King Lear's misrecognition, at the end of the play, is that Cordelia is still alive. Othello is the best example, perhaps, seeing no fault in himself, but thinking that he 'loved not wisely but too well'. And another misrecognition is John's discovery in *Oleanna*.

At the end of the play, when Carol presents her list of demands, John suddenly becomes assertive and reverses from the beaten person he was before to discover a new understanding of his purpose in life:

> I want to tell you something. I'm a teacher. I am a teacher. Eh? It's my *name* on the door, and I teach the class, and that's what I do. I've got a *book* with my name on it. And my son will see that book someday. And I have a respon . . . No, I'm sorry . . . I have a *responsibility* . . . to *myself*, to my *son*, to my *profession* . . . (76)

There are many ironies here. This belated discovery of his true mission shows no responsibility to his students at all. Instead, he is still totally oriented to himself.

The most substantive scholarly dispute involves the final lines of the play which truncate the ending. Brenda Murphy (2004) surveys the debate in her masterful essay on *Oleanna*. The final lines are as ambiguous as the play itself, open to multiple interpretations, in contrast to the first draft which Pinter staged in London which explicitly gave the victory to Carol, and a recantation to John. Murphy observes that 'most critics agree with Richard Badenhausen's conclusion that it is a "chilling acknowledgment" of John's misogynistic rhetoric' (1998: 134). She notes others agree with Thomas Porter that 'it is "not immediately clear what Carol is affirming"' (134).

And she cites Thomas Goggans' view of it as confirmation of a back-story of sexual abuse. Murphy, however, argues that

> The ending indicates that Carol's empowerment through the feminist language of her Group has been an illusion, just as has John's empowerment through the language of academia. He is reduced to spewing abuse and beating up a woman because he is stronger than she, and she is reduced to accepting him in his hateful and demeaning word, despite the fact that the linguistic code of the law empowers her to put him in jail. (2004: 135–6)

Thus Carol loses as much as John does, and it is a tragedy for both of them, in Murphy's reading, restoring a sense of balance to the play.

What is key is that in erasing the overly explicit Pinter ending, Mamet's production is true to the play which leaves it to the viewer to interpret. Another way to take the passage is that when Carol says, 'Yes, that's right,' she is reacting to his line: 'I wouldn't touch you with a ten foot pole, cunt . . .' Her view is that this is his only category for her, and his last line confirms it. It could also be that her lines are a response to his concluding line: (*She cowers on the floor below him. Pause. He looks down at her. He lowers the chair. He moves to his desk, and arranges the papers on it. Pause. He looks over at her.*) '. . . well . . .' (80). Does his 'well' mean, 'Well, I've really done it now?' That's one option. If this were the case, her lines are actually delivered first to him, then to herself. 'Yes. That's right.' (*She looks away from him, and lowers her head. To herself.*) '. . . yes. That's right' (80). At first she's agreeing with him – yes, you've really destroyed your life now; yes, you've really proved you are what I said you were.

But by repeating the line to herself, she is clearly not fully convinced and needs to assert her rightness again. This is a reminder of Perry's idea of the dualistic framework. Carol is vindicated, in her view, for she was 'right'. And John was 'wrong'. But more sophisticated frameworks exist for the audience which has viewed the play. And we should be able to see that people don't have fixed identities, are not simply 'right' or 'wrong' as Carol thinks. Rather, they are inter-active, as John argues. And while he thinks of himself as a successful teacher and academic, he is unconsciously patriarchal and patroniz-ing. But when Carol's charges are accepted, and he loses tenure and ultimately his house and job, he becomes what she says he is. That is, in this play, the tragedy results from people being what others see them as being. At the beginning of the play, Carol is a failure because her teacher says she's a failure; John is a failure as a teacher because his student says he's a sexist failure at the end of the play. And that is what he becomes. But this full dimension of the tragedy is never recognized by either character. Perhaps only the audience can see that both are wrong in their constructions of themselves and of the other. But, after, all, 'we can only interpret the behavior of others through the screen we [. . .] create' (19–20).

Changing views of the play

Mamet's playwriting approach is to challenge the audience (and actors) with unresolved lacunae. Matthew Roudané, in *American Drama Since 1960*, has given an excellent analysis of what I am call-ing postmodern realistic form as a series of 'gaps' in the realistic veneer that should be used as the basis for any analysis of the play:

> The play is theatrically powerful precisely because its author never fills in such gaps. Instead, the theatergoer thinks, Is Carol framing John? Are her accusations legitimate? Is Carol simply the first to have the courage to challenge a patronizing and, perhaps, womanizing male teacher? Is John so much a part of an inherently misogynistic world that he is blithely unaware that his well-meaning actions are in fact highly sexist? Mamet invites the audience to respond to these and many other issues [. . .].
> (Roudané, 1997: 173)

The passage makes clear that the questions of meani
often raised concerning this play are precipitated not by
that Mamet gives to these questions, but rather by the way the play
avoids them. As a result the audience, assuming the play to be realistic, fills in the gaps for the playwright with sometimes quite forced
or bizarre results.

The clearest example of how these gaps work is Francine Russo's
essay from the *Village Voice* which alternates between trying to see
the play objectively, as an equal contest, and her gut-feeling that it
is all woman-bashing:

> Alternate programs were printed, half showing a male figure with
> a target on his chest, the other half with a female sporting the
> same bull's eye. A contest of perception. [. . .] But it was always
> a rigged game. There's been a lot of smart analysis of this play to
> prove it's weighted on both sides, but to experience *Oleanna*, you
> need to bring your nose as well as your intellect. The on-its-head
> world Mamet's written reeks of woman-hating, and his director-
> ial choices spew a mean-spirited, unwholesome smog over the
> proceedings on and off-stage. (Russo, 1993: 96–7)

The jump within one paragraph, which begins with the marketing
strategy of equal programs, then leaps to her perception, demonstrates the kind of back and forth moves that Russo makes. Her
language and diction provide a microcosm of the whole controversy.

Academic critics also fall into the trap of filling in the gaps on
their own. Roger Bechtel fills in the gap of 'the Group' to produce
his view of Carol: 'The Group has subsumed her identity into its
own, and she has become as rigid and unforgiving as it must be'
(1996: 39). Stephen Ryan, who otherwise takes a balanced approach
to the play, sees John as 'the catalyst who drives her into the arms of
the "group", who minister to her bewilderment by providing a
comfortable illusion of certainty that renders her confusion about
the academic world completely comprehensible' (1996: 396).

Russo recognizes the characterization of Carol as a similarly empty signifier, as well as how the gaps in the narrative are filled by different interpreters:

> But Carol is at best insufferable, at worst antiseptically evil. She's a cipher, a trick card, an either/or. You can project anything you like upon her, as the critics have. Can you see *Oleanna* as 'a tragedy of language,' as the *Voice*'s Michael Feingold does? Yeah, you can. Can you make a case, as John Lahr does in *The New Yorker*, that it's about 'the awful spoiling power of envy disguised as political ideology'? Why not? These interpretations are built partly on character, and viewers can just jot what they like in the character blank. *The Times*'s David Richards concedes Mamet 'is not exactly playing fair' and 'forces us to chart our own path through the play with only our speculations and prejudices to guide us.' Sure. Leave some pieces out of a puzzle and people will fill in the holes. A good Rorschach test, perhaps, but hardly proof of literary merit. (1993: 97)

This excerpt clearly depicts what Mamet has given – a puzzle with missing pieces, and yet what Russo has made of it is clear from the earlier passages. Russo is evidently aware of the existence of the gaps, and yet can't help herself from constructing her view of Carol which she knows is a projection of her own psyche, a Rorschach test. This is most honest. Her quotations from reviewers make clear the variety of ways the gaps are filled. The quotation from Richards indicates how the play forces the audience to project its own prejudices onto the characters, as in Russo's essay.

Mamet encourages the audience to misinterpret the play as Russo does by presenting the play as a seemingly realistic construction, which can then be interpreted by realistic rules. But when the audience applies those rules, instead of objectivity there is subjective prejudice that mirrors one's own interpretation. Thus Mamet's gaps allow the audience to experience something like what Russo experiences: an externalization of its own fears, and a recognition that the characters are not at all what one thinks they are. The framework which one assumes determines how the object is seen and understood. The objective reality of the characters in *Oleanna* cannot be seen except through one framework or another – so it is one's own constructs one confronts when watching the play: 'We can only interpret the behavior of others through the screen we . . . Through the screen we create' (19–20). There is at least a double irony in this line: John says it condescendingly to Carol as if she alone misunderstands him because of faulty screening. But the irony is developed in the second act, when the Tenure Committee accepts her construction of the first act episode, so Carol's 'screen' becomes the dominant. An added level of irony, however, is that the audience too interprets the play as a whole 'Through the screen we create'.

New York reviewers split along lines that have continued virtually to the present. Generally, there were three responses to the play. One group thought John was mistreated, and saw the play as his tragedy (Henry III, Lahr, Barnes). Another, mainly feminist in origin, were outraged by the treatment of Carol and upset with the accusation of rape, seeing Mamet as failing to be even-handed, and so mistreating women (Rich, Solomon, Stuart). A third group found the handling to be balanced in its examination of the abuse of power, whoever is in charge (Feingold, Kroll, Weales).

Most critics were outraged at John's mistreatment by Carol, likening her and her third act costume to the Chinese Red Guard (Lahr, Rich, Solomon). But Kroll saw: 'On the surface, her accusations seem frightening in their lethal absurdity. But inexorably we realize that she is telling the truth – her truth. His compliments ("Don't you look fetching") she sees as sexist put-downs coming from his position of power' (1992: 65).

Nearly all faulted Mamet's direction of the play because they saw the actors as underplaying emotion. That is, the actors didn't display emotion when and where the reviewer expected it – to conform to his or her interpretation of the play. Barnes and Sterritt both saw 'ritual' in Mamet's direction of the performances, and several saw a 'debate'. Simon, Barnes, and Watt noticed the 'spare' staging, but none drew any significance from the lack of a realistic set.

The British reviewers focused more on the performances than the issues, which had become familiar, perhaps, from the New York premier. Mamet's production lasted 90 minutes; the printed Royal Court script (Methuen) lists one intermission and the play to last 2 hours and 10 minutes in the Pinter directed production. In addition, Pinter's set filled the stage with greater specificity than Mamet used. But reviewers who had seen the New York production were nearly unanimous in praising this one as superior because Pinter's production had 'more balance and ambiguity in the piece' (Taylor, 1993: 743). David Suchet was lauded for showing the 'smugness' and self-satisfied flawed side of John; Lia Williams was praised for showing the shift from first act to second between genuine bewilderment to become a 'fury' (Rutherford, 1993: 742). Marvin, however, noted that she was too 'gorgeous. The girl must be a sexless spinster or the play is thrown off balance.' But Wolf countered that with his view that: 'Whereas Mamet directed [. . .] Carol as a prim, sexless, schoolmarm, Pinter understands that the play is much more disturbing if her gathering confidence allows Carol to develop a sexuality as well as a case' (Wolf, 1993: 77).

Pinter used the first draft in which Carol totally defeated John: 'Carol gets up from the vicious assault and finds the confession she wants him to deliver before the whole school and list of books (including his own) the Group wants banned. The broken man is reading this out to her as the play ends' (Taylor). Aleks Sierz explains how Pinter improved Mamet: 'By sympathising so overtly with John, Mamet turns this trial of strength into a kangaroo court. [. . .] Although the play's ideological deck is stacked, this version (brilliantly directed by Harold Pinter, who underlines the play's language games) restores Mamet's original ending with its deep sensation of failure' (1993: 740).

Hersh Zeifman, in *The David Mamet Review,* also saw Pinter's version as an improvement seesawing audience sympathy:

> Lia Williams's Carol was far more human, and therefore believable, than her New York counterpart – frightened and vulnerable in her initial helplessness, smug and arrogant as she slowly inched her way toward a painful, exultant, and decidedly Pyrrhic 'victory.' Similarly, David Suchet captured wonderfully the paradoxes and ambiguity of John; his surface generosity and concern could not entirely mask an underlying unctuousness and condescension that were deeply disturbing. Carol's battle for psychic 'territory' was reflected in Pinter's gradually allowing her to claim more and more physical space. (Zeifman, 1994: 1)

Scholarly disputes reflect readings like that of the British production in which Carol is not a cipher, but a real person. When she is taken thus realistically, critics assume Mamet's misogyny (Bean, Burkman, Garner, McDonough and Silverstein). Others look at the play with more detachment, rather than taking it as real. They look at the thematic issues, seeking to understand the play's contribution to current disputes over sexual harassment and political correctness (Piette). A third group looks at abuses of power and/or the nature of language (Bechtel, Elam, Kane), and who has the power to interpret it (Jean Jacques Weber). Those who argue the power theme are more sensitive to Carol's motivation (Badenhausen, Foster, Goggans, Hardin, Ryan). Those who argue misogyny usually base the argument on the lack of a perceived motive/reason for the change in Carol between Act One and Act Two. If there is no motive, then Carol is a 'two-dimensional' character and not a serious characterization. There is also concern that Mamet's use of Carol's charge of rape is a trivialization of a serious issue. Those who sympathize with Carol sometimes argue that she has the motivations of a realistic character (Goggans) and tend to ascribe her motives to 'her group' (Mason); but some see her as other than realistic – postmodern and performative (Elam, MacLeod, Porter, Sauer, and Skloot).

But the central problem of the play has not been fully addressed: how and why does this play alone inflame such passionate and divided responses? Heather Braun, surveying Mamet's plays of 'The 1990s', notes that Mamet sought to explain that 'both characters believed they were correct and that the strength of their righteousness is what ultimately brings about their destruction. Such assertions, however, failed even to tone down angry responses from playgoers who, like the characters of Mamet's plays, also resorted to verbal and physical violence against actors and each other after numerous performances' (2004: 108). What critical surveys fail to acknowledge is that despite the argument that the play is too one-sided, in fact the audience divides into two camps, not one. And what is fascinating is that, like the characters, each side thinks it is right and the other wrong.

Perhaps as a result, more recently the most common approach to the play is to sidestep both audience response and the political and social issues, and focus instead on its pedagogical dimension. Richard C. Raymond uses the play both to analyse the rhetoric and to train students in how to marshal evidence of their own to support arguments, indicating the new direction of research. Raymond uses the play as an example of how not to teach, as well as to help students recognize how and why disagreements among rational people can occur.

Stan Garner argues 'that the play was harnessing outrage to a gender politics that it does little to question' (2000: 39). In order to remedy this, he taught the play in conjunction with his university's production. He planned discussion to explore those assumptions of gender politics he saw as unexamined. However, the students resisted his efforts; they identified with John, while he attempted to defend Carol with whom they had no sympathy. 'Whatever strategies I might have tried to teach against Mamet's play, I would have had to admit both the limits of classroom framing and the powerful cultural pressures conditioning student response' (2000: 49). In Garner's view, the play is too slanted towards John, for he could not sway his students to see Carol's point of view.

Robert Skloot finds a fruitful approach using Paolo Frière in 'Oleanna, or, the Play of Pedagogy'. Skloot has a balanced recognition that 'Carol's pedagogy is as repressive as his [John's] own' (2001: 99). Both are seen to conform to Frière's teacher as oppressor.

More often the play is used as an example of bad teaching. Dale M. Bauer uses the film version to fit a larger thesis: 'Indecent Proposals: Teachers in the Movies.' Here the play is seen as an indicator of subconscious psychological interactions between teacher and student raising issues of gender. Jo Keroes also explores gender and teaching. Geraldine Shipton goes further into the psychological relationship in 'The Annihilation of Triangular Space'. Donna Dunbar-Odom uses Oleanna to examine interaction of student and Composition teacher.

These studies have advanced understanding of teacher–student interactions in terms of sexuality, psychology and spatial arrangement, and as a consequence, have added new dimensions to recognizing the multiple contexts of Oleanna. Despite these advances, understanding of the play in terms of polarizing an audience and provoking controversy has not substantially improved. Writers still lament that their students identify with the faculty member, not with the student; faculty still tend to favour the student over the teacher. This reversal of expected identification, however, has not resulted in any deeper recognition of how or why audience members identify with one position or another. And the crucial fact that well-intentioned people react totally differently needs better explanation, both as to how and why such responses so polarize into binaries.

3 Production History

This chapter is a brief history of productions of *Oleanna*. It looks at the original 1992 ART production in Cambridge, Massachusetts which moved to the New York Orpheum Theater in October, then to Washington DC's Kennedy Center in May 1993, and the London production of Harold Pinter at the Royal Court June, 1993, as well as Mamet's film version, 1994.

Minimalism in Mamet's original production

Although no one has yet explored in depth Mamet's relation to the minimalist art movement, minimalism is crucial to understand his work in performance. At the First International David Mamet Conference in Las Vegas, William Macy recounted acting in Mamet's film *Homicide* in which he played the cop-sidekick to Joe Mantegna. The film centres on Mantegna's Bob Gould's discovery of his roots and Jewish identity. Macy says he was in a scene in which he was filling out a passport application, and his line was 'Bob, I *am* your family' (80). Realizing the line is crucial to the meaning of the film's identity theme, Macy looked up at Mantegna and said the line meaningfully. Mamet stopped the filming and said, 'Just fill out the paperwork, Bill.' So Macy did another take, not looking up, but saying the line again meaningfully, '"Cut, cut", said Mamet. "Just fill out the paperwork, Bill."' And the third time, Macy said the line without any intonation, just filling out the paperwork. And that is the take that is in the film, and works best, according to Macy.

The lesson to be learned is that Mamet acting is minimalist, underplayed. Mamet assumes intelligence and active engagement by the audience. In his most successful films like *House of Games* and *Spanish Prisoner*, fragmentary con games require the audience's participation at every step to guess what is coming next, who is conning whom. And so Mamet's ideal actor is one who does not overplay emotion, or even emote. Rather, in Mamet's view, the work of the playwright is dominant and his job is to create a situation which seethes with emotion, and the audience should not need actors embellishing the text with feelings, explicitly revealing how the character feels. The situation should show the character, and the audience by its participation fills in the feeling.

Mamet's approach to acting, like his approach to writing, is not to fill in the past history of the character and enact an inner life on stage; quite the opposite as he argues in *True and False*:

> The Method got it wrong. Yes, the actor is undergoing something on stage, but it is beside the point to have him or her 'undergo' the supposed trials of the character upon the stage. The actor has his own trials to undergo, and they are right in front of him. They don't have to be superadded; they exist. His challenge is not to recapitulate, to *pretend* to the difficulties of the written character; it is to open the mouth, stand straight, and say the words bravely – adding nothing, denying nothing, and without the intent to manipulate anyone: himself, his fellows, the audience. (Mamet, 1997: 22)

This is the lesson Mamet taught Macy in *Homicide*.

Mamet's theory of acting, however, can be a little baffling to the actor and to the newcomer. Perhaps a better place to explain *Oleanna*'s minimalism is to examine the visual, for that is the dimension readers who have not seen Mamet's production might find more difficult to imagine or grasp. Seeing the film of the play doesn't help, unfortunately. Macy told me that he and David [Mamet] can't figure out why the film didn't have the impact that the play had. It had the same actors. It had the same lines. It had the same writer/director. But it caused none of the controversy. Why?

My answer is that the film is, visually, the antithesis of the play. The film is overly decorated – the untenured professor has a lush office that would put many College Presidents' offices to shame. Ironically, the film was shot at an abandoned mental institution in Massachusetts that was supposed to convey, one assumes, the view of the song 'Oleanna' about the Norwegian utopian community. Instead, the opening song is a sweet kind of Alma Mater. The first shots depict idyllic students playing on the lawns before columned buildings. The irony is that higher education is a failed utopia. But the film's setting is so plush that the message is obscured. Worse, being set in a real place, it makes the story a minor anecdote about a real student and professor, and so of no larger significance. It is not a depiction of stereotypes in our own heads, and about unearthing deep-seated cultural fears. By taking away the audience's imaginative engagement, the realm of the play shifts from inner psychology to outer incident.

Reviewers were also puzzled over why the film failed to have the impact of the play. After analyzing the play, Roger Ebert concludes: 'Would the film seem more powerful to someone unfamiliar with the play? I obviously have no way of knowing. All I can say is that Mamet's play, so provoking that I bought and read the script, doesn't seem to have the same effect on the screen' (1994: 26). Ron Weiskind thought Mamet must have tried to record the stage version and wound up with one that was 'mummified' (1994: B6). Mamet's screenplays are in great demand, leading to big Hollywood success, an Oscar nomination for his early *The Verdict,* and commissions for blockbusters like *Wag the Dog* and the second Hannibal Lecter movie, *Hannibal.* But when his plays are made into films, they have little impact, except for James Foley's film of *Glengarry*

Glen Ross. American Buffalo, Lakeboat, The Water Engine, A Life in the Theatre, and *Edmond* have been made into films, but have been largely unsuccessful.

Contrast the film with the play's setting in Mamet's original production. It was minimalist in an extreme – a 20-foot square raised platform, the only part of the stage illuminated. There were no walls or doors. There were two benches along the stage right side, an opening for a door upstage right, and fragmentary wainscoting along the back wall and a bit of the up left wall. Into that corner, angled, was John's desk with chair. In front of the desk was a wooden chair with another along the left side. That was the whole set. From the outset, the audience has to imagine it as an office, and is engaged actively. From that point on, the audience participates, as it does in Mamet's film/mysteries, trying to figure out the next move.

At first glance, Mamet's production of the play seemed realistic in costumes and acting. Yet the set sent the opposite signal because of its minimalist lack of realism. Clive Barnes was dismayed at its barrenness:

> The physical production (it took 13 producers to raise the money for this!) looks so Spartanly bare (even chintzy – and not in the English sense) that it appears more suitable for a read-through than a staging. Adding to the anti-theatrical chill Mamet himself has directed his actors [. . .] into a stylized ritual, effetely artificial in phrase and pause, halfway between debate and conflict but irreversibly frozen. (1992: 359)

Barnes recognized the 'anti-theatrical' elements of the bare set and stylized acting, but not how these elements play off of the realistic costumes, language and action. In Bertolt Brecht's theatre, A-effects such as songs, signs, supertitles were designed to interrupt the audience's engagement, and keep the audience from simply passively observing, feeling. He sought instead to jar the audience continually,

to think as well as to feel. Mamet's style of production works similarly, the set operating in opposition to the seeming realism of the
characters and dialogue. But the play's set, costumes, and blocking
all were carefully chosen to convey meaning. David Barbour dis-
cussed the production ingredients with Harriet Voyt, Mamet's
assistant and concluded of *Oleanna*:

> Written in the appropriately elusive Mametian style, the mini-
> malist design [. . .] is nonetheless filled with telling details. 'I've
> [Voyt] worked for David for a few years now; we talked about
> how the characters should look.' Because of the overall minimal
> approach, she notes, every detail was given extra weight. 'We'd
> go through everything', she says. 'We'd take a look at the socks
> and say, "We have to change those"'. (1993: 8)

What was done, especially for *Oleanna* which Mamet himself
directed, has a fixity that provides a foundation for other approaches
to the play. This is especially an authorized version because Mamet's
wife, Rebecca Pidgeon, played Carol, and William H. Macy, who
had worked with Mamet continuously since being taught by him in
college twenty years before, played John. There could not be more
sympathy between cast and director, and so their production is
definitive in a way that few others in dramatic history have been.
The 20 January 1993 performance is preserved on videotape at the
New York Public Library for the Performing Arts.

Under Mamet's direction, Macy only goes behind the desk to
talk on the telephone. He does not use it as a spatial barrier between
himself and Carol. At the outset, when he is on the phone, she sits
in the opposite corner, downstage right, on the bench. He is in
control of the space and usually she is stage right near the entrance/
exit ready to flee. He is physically identified with the desk, again his
place of power. He leans against the front of it, stands behind it to
answer the phone and talk, and rarely sits on the desk. In the second

act, to demonstrate the reversal of power, his first place to sit is on her bench. She takes the chair and sits opposite him. Physically this makes clear the shift in power and position that has happened between the acts.

This production makes *Oleanna* a play of simple reversal from the first act to the second. Carol is inarticulate and scared in the first act, and very assertive and confident in the second. Part of the cause of her inability to speak, however, is that Macy's John keeps cutting her off. He is clearly used to working with inarticulate students who stammer and are unable to express clearly what they want to say, and he leaps ahead of her, finishes her sentences, and then answers what he thinks was going to be her point. So she keeps trying to say things, 'I – I – I', but is never allowed to complete them. My sense is that the opening especially needs to be played extremely quickly, as she tries to speak, he cuts her off, and they exchange fragmentary thoughts as stichomythia (exchange of single lines back and forth).

In the second act, however, John goes from being powerful and fully confident, to losing confidence, becoming inarticulate, and finally fizzling out, defeated – only to rise from the ashes with the violence of the final attack. In the first act, Carol is constantly asking for definitions of words – clearly she is lost and cannot understand. Partly this is simply due to vocabulary. In fact, when John gets lost in his own reflection on the difference between 'heterodoxy' and 'orthodoxy', the audience laughs at him (there are, in fact, a number of laughs in the first half of the play in this live performance recording). In the second half, however, she is the one in charge of language – she interrupts him to point out how he misuses words: 'These are not accusations, they've been proven as facts.'

The hinge words for the reversal seem to be, 'I don't understand' (the word 'understand' is used 35 times in the play, 24 of those negatively, 'I don't understand'). The character who says this is the person without power who is struggling to catch up. And the one who does understand never hesitates to lecture the one who is powerless about how simple the ideas are to grasp. Lines can be found to chart this reversal of power.

Costumes in this production are similarly emblematic, rather than realistic. The play begins with John in sweater and blue shirt and tie – comfortable and at home with his power and position. The sweater is a massive brown cardigan which simultaneously builds him up, and also says that he is relaxed, not suited but at ease. Carol is in glasses, initially in a shapeless, sleeveless shift, a brown baggy long dress with a dark mock turtleneck underneath and a white shirt over that. She wears white socks and perhaps Dr. Martens, black tie shoes. The impression is of a little girl, perhaps to convey innocence.

In Act Two, these costumes are completely changed. He is in a dark suit and tie – apparently ready to testify before the Tenure Committee. But instead of this giving him more power, it gives him less. He is not dressing for comfort, but in the costume of the power structure against which he likes to define himself. Carol is in a unisex costume: simple dark green chinos, the turtleneck, and a beige vest. She takes off a tweed overcoat. These costumes are a transition to the third act where the contrast is completely clear. She is in a near pants suit: dark blazer with an emblem, almost matching colour pants, white shirt. He is in shirt and tie only – and the tie knot is slid down almost off the lower end, the top two shirt buttons are undone. All of it says that he is dissolving, and has become stripped of almost all emblems of power and position. The tie is hanging on by a thread. Finally when the thread snaps, however, it is psychologically, rather than physically.

The blocking, too, demonstrates this shift of power. In the first act, he is in total control of the movement. Macy takes a chair and places it just across from the bench right. But he doesn't offer her a seat – she takes the bench as he first sits in the chair. At other times he moves the straight wooden chair around the set, sometimes to sit opposite her, sometimes to place it centre and put her in the middle. In the second act to demonstrate the reversal of power, his first place to sit is on her bench. She takes the chair and sits opposite him. Physically this makes clear the psychological change of power and position that has happened between the two acts.

The crucial elements in staging, however, are the moments of physical touching. The Act One moment clearly defines John's view of Carol. She puts on her coat and tries to escape. He stops her, physically, at the door, takes her coat off of her, turns her around with his hand on her shoulder, and then conveys her to the centre of the room where he deposits her in a chair. This is when he makes his offer of the A if she will just come and see him and work through this problem of lack of understanding. Physically he has totally taken charge of her.

Later in the act, however, she is not so submissive. He is joking about the Tenure Committee finding out his 'dark secret', essentially that he is unworthy of the position, as his family had told him in the past. She wants to know what the secret is, and he dismisses it laughingly. She quickly shifts ground to ask about her grade but the phone rings. After that interruption, Macy goes towards her, both are standing, and she backs up until she has nowhere left to turn – between the two benches stage right. Pidgeon then turns away towards the door and they freeze momentarily, with their backs to the audience as he puts his arm around her shoulders. When this happens, she jumps and spins quickly under his arm. He asks, 'What do you feel?' and the meaning is highly ambiguous. To him it is the usual Carl Rogers non-directive psychological counselling question. But the feelings she has had when he put his arm around her may be quite different. 'I feel bad. [. . .] I don't understand you. [. . .] I can't tell you. [. . .] I'm bad. [. . .] I have never told anyone this . . .' (37–8). As she is about to tell him her deepest secret – they seem to have reached a place of real confiding and understanding – the telephone rings, the party is announced, and he must leave. He never notices what is happening. Seemingly the physical touch has aroused something in her, something she is about to confess for the first time. He simply ignores all the feelings he had triggered in her, and the act ends.

Clearly he just doesn't get it – he never sees anything sexual about the contact, but it does have some effect on her that he ignores. And when he pleads at the start of the second act, 'What have I done to you? How can I make amends?' he sounds convincing, having no clue as to what he has done.

Another major shift of the second act is the change in pitch of her voice. Pidgeon begins the play with a very high pitched, little girl voice. In the second act it is normal to low pitched, and in the third even lower. When she says 'Good day', leaving at the end of the first scene of the second act, it is a husky almost masculine voice.

The reversal is apparent in the second act when she exclaims, 'I don't care what you feel!' after he has gone on and on about his feelings, without ever recognizing that this very word was what brought her to the brink of confessing her tormenting secret, only to be ignored and rebuffed by a phone call. After the exclamation, she drives him back to sit on the bench, and is fully empowered. Now she cuts him off. The line, 'Professor, to refer to the Committee as Good Men and True, it is a demeaning remark. It is a sexist remark' is delivered with her standing and him sitting, the complete opposite of the first act. At this point he exclaims, 'I'm not the subject. (*Pause.*) And where I'm wrong . . . perhaps it's not your job to "fix" me' (53). What is fascinating about this declaration, coming as it does right after the reversal of his sexist 'Good Men and True', is that the battle between them is about who is in charge of defining meaning, who is the subject and who is the object?

Traditional male criticism has assumed that there was one fixed objective centre to the universe, one that otherized women and minorities of all kinds, subjects to be scrutinized and examined with detachment. It is this stance that Professor John assumes without question. And though he tries to question the status quo, he never challenges this basic assumption, nor does he ever take gender (or race, or anything else not in his own experience) into account. That is why the power is so easily reversed. His final response, the traditional male response, is to use force – finally pushing her into a chair as she tries to leave, grabbing her forcibly so that she cries for help. His doom is complete.

From the outset it is clear that Carol does not want to be touched. It makes her extremely uncomfortable, and she jumps or shies away each time he nears her. Is that because she was abused as a child? Or is it because she is attracted to the professor and fights against it? Or because she has an aversion to men? The point is emphasized in the production when Macy moves towards Pidgeon on 'There's no one here but you and me.' As he does, she keeps backing away until she hits the bench, then holds both hands out in front of her, to yell 'All right. I did not understand' and he then backs away, gets a chair, and sits. He is not threatening, but her reaction implies she thinks he is. We cannot know what causes these reactions. But the fact that she is uncomfortable is totally unobserved by John, and it comes as no surprise that he physically attacks her at the end of the play because so much of the play has depended on the physical interaction, and on the gap between their two kinds of understanding.

John finally shouts in the last scene what has been evident from the beginning: 'I don't understand!' She tries to explain it to him: 'To lay a hand on someone's shoulder' – he cuts her off 'It was devoid of sexual content!' She punches out the key point: 'IT IS NOT FOR YOU TO SAY!' (70). This has been the issue throughout the play, and polling the audience at the end as was done in Washington, DC, is a perfect way to make clear to the audience that there is no objectivity to their judgements – and to problematize the key issue of the play. Who is to decide who is object and who is subject, who is scrutinized and to be taught, and who gets to be the teacher?

Although Macy told me the Kennedy Center management suggested the blackboard, Mamet must have approved it. What does the blackboard imply? First, it announces to the audience that, as the *Oleanna* film poster warned, 'Whatever side you take, you're wrong.' Clearly some people sympathize with John, some with Carol. And seeing that choice on a blackboard problematizes the response for everyone. It is a *post-facto* way to get the audience to confront the postmodern point of the play – that it is our own stereotypes we see on stage, more than what is really there. The even more ironic middle question asks the question about realism: does the audience take this play as if it were reality?

As Rosenfeld reported percentages varied depending on the audience. Matinee audiences voted with him much more strongly – and virtually all thought it could really happen. But the key to this poll is that as an audience member I was shocked at how many disagreed. The de-centring of the audience, of interpretation, happens in the moment one confronts the blackboard, or hears the disputes which ensue after the performance.

In the indeterminate postmodern play, there are different contexts in which different audience members read the text. The result is that the play *Oleanna* is not about John and Carol, the characters, so much as it is about how we read John and Carol. If we assume that we 'know' Carol in an objective and unbiased way, as we are led to think we 'know' realism's characters, we are in error. Carol's innermost secret is never revealed, and so any interpretation made of her is necessarily a subjective, not objective, construction. She is not, finally, knowable in the complete sense that realistic characters are.

Why would Mamet withdraw from an author's power and authority over his text? Macy provides his answer as he gives his truth to Liane Hansen:

> They [the audience] just can't accept what they see before their very eyes. They want to figure it out, well, what's the angle. They

just can't accept that it's a professor who is very full of himself and is biting the hand that feeds him, when it comes to the educational system and the university. (Hansen, 1993)

Macy is close to Mamet's point here – but in fact it is the system itself which subverts and distorts the people within it. When the professor has control and power, he is distorted by the system; when the student has it, she is as well. The fault is not in the individual psychology of each character, as it would have been in modernist realism, but rather in the system as a whole.

Acting Mamet

For the Mamet actor playing Carol the approach to the confession cannot be the conventional, Method-based, realistic assumption of an inner life to the character. Instead, character is all on the surface, and the actor need only deliver the lines. Because it is open-ended and never fully explained, this kind of confession is truly ambivalent, or multivalent. In such a case, the actor sends no signals to the audience of the hidden inner life. The audience is left to puzzle out its own interpretation of the character, with no direction from the actor, as *True and False* indicates:

The actor does not need to 'become' the character. The phrase, in fact, has no meaning. There is no character. There are only lines upon a page. They are lines of dialogue meant to be said by the actor. When he or she says them simply, in an attempt to achieve an object more or less like that suggested by the author, the audience sees the illusion of a character upon the stage. (1997: 9)

Just as the actor need not become the character, or fill in the 'subtext', so too the Mamet audience need not look for hidden meanings, the inner life of the characters, as was done in modernist realism. The focus of the play is not to hold a mirror up to nature, as a realist would have done, but to hold it up to the audience itself making clear how the audience's own preconceptions are mirrored in the way the characters and action are understood.

The function of ambiguity in modernist realistic drama, therefore, is to give space for the actor to make choices. It also leaves space for the discerning reader, or viewer, to perceive a larger view than that of the more didactic, single-minded reader. The result still privileges the audience, giving it the sense of objectivity and perception of the grand narrative. In the de-centred ambivalence of the postmodern dramatist, however, that place of actor and audience privilege is gone. Both are given merely the words on the page, and any construction of depth, subtext, or inner life is a construction of the actor/audience, rather than of the play itself. The play instead, like the reality it seeks to present, is constructed of indeterminacy and mocks any attempt to reduce it to neat choices or ambiguities.

In performance, an audience forms a temporary community and responds, usually, with a kind of unanimity. And yet every night's audience responds somewhat differently. The exact same community is never formed. Mamet seems to be exploiting this fact by creating a play whose meaning not only depends on the variations in response, but even encourages them. Its effect, then, seems to require discussing these variations after the performance, if not as a group, at least with those with whom one attended the play.

To attempt to interpret *Oleanna* by the standards and approaches of modernism can only lead to frustration. Limiting critical choices to the simple either/or of modernist dichotomy results in the critic's having to choose between Carol and John, and to build a case around one choice. But the ambivalence of indeterminacy requires that much greater space be left open in interpreting the postmodern work. Character's motives are not fully knowable, as they are in the revealed-secret form of modernist realism. And the interpreter must recognize that postmodern characters are not fully knowable. If the critic can accept that, then a different kind of appreciation of the art of the dramatist will result.

4 Workshopping *Oleanna*

This chapter offers a series of practical workshop exercises based on *Oleanna*. It involves discussion of the play's characters, conflicts, key scenes, motifs and ideas which a group of student actors could explore practically for themselves. The content is also informed by interviews with actors and directors who have been involved in professional productions of the play.

The words of the play as gibberish

In the interview with Liane Hansen, William H. Macy explains the play:

> David's [Mamet's] point of view, and I believe he's exactly right, is there it is, it's on the page, it's right in front of you. You don't need to know any back story. And I always find it fascinating that audiences come in to this play and because it's such a hot button issue, and they bring so much anger to the party that they have a tendency to want to interpret the play. [. . .] That's what's presented and that's from David's point of view, that's all there is. What you see is what you get. There's no hidden meaning in this play. (Hansen, 1993)

In Macy's view, the words are on the page. They require no director to fill in hidden meanings. But the audience, raised on conventional realism, automatically starts to fill in the gaps, projecting their own anger into the situation. (Even Macy, as he denies doing it, gives his own construction of the Group: '[. . .] it is natural that she would glom onto a group that would embrace her fears and say, "here is an answer to the questions that you have. You're being shafted by men, by the university, by this professor in particular" '. But none of this is in the play.) The words on the page are all there is.

Macy emphasizes this point when Hansen observes, 'The dialogue itself, in many instances, nothing is really said':

I think you have to play the dialogue as if it's gibberish. The only thing that you can play, I think in all plays, but particularly in David's plays, you can't make it mean something. What you've got to do is be clear on what the objective is or another way to put it, is be clear what you want from the other person and get the other person to do that and let the lines speak as they will. They're just gibberish. (Hansen, 1993)

It is hard to imagine any other actor regarding the playwright's words as 'gibberish' but this is the Mamet/Macy school of acting. There are moment-by-moment goals which the actor must find to focus on the character's intentions. But the literal words are probably not direct expressions of the intention.

This is a postmodern approach to acting, writing and character, since it does not promulgate the modernist's hidden, unconscious motives for action – the Freudian unconscious is abandoned. Stanislavsky's method, which dominated American acting for most of the twentieth century similarly built from within the character's psyche and the actor's. But Mamet's approach to character is totally different:

There's no such thing as 'character.' 'Character' doesn't exist. If you take a piece of writing, what you're going to see is twelve to twenty lines on a page for a hundred and twenty pages. If you turn it upside down, nothing's going to fall out. There isn't any 'character' there. It's a bunch of words that people say, period. That's what Aristotle told us, and it's true today. There's no such thing as 'character.' It's just little words that the writer made up. (Mamet on Playwriting, 1993: 10)

Given Mamet's view, one wonders why critics continue to treat him as if he were a conventional realistic playwright. But as Macy indicates, audiences fill in the gaps in the narrative and make real people out of the fragmentary characters. In Mamet's view, the characters are not real people, as they were viewed in realism, but rather are simply words on a page, just as the setting is not a reality, but a fragment. Actors and audiences make a mistake if they try to make them too real.

Approaching *Oleanna* through performance

If acting in or directing *Oleanna*, there is one huge problem: how to avoid taking sides. The argument of this book has been that audience members are easily drawn into Mamet's game. His point is that 'whatever side you take, you're wrong.' For the *Playbill*, for the first time in history, there were two covers: one with a male figure seated, in front of a target; one with a female figure in front of a target. Mamet has done all he can to make the point that choosing one side or the other is mistaken.

For the actor, of course, there is no surprise here. Whatever character one plays, the typical advice is to learn not to caricature, which results from judging one's character, but rather to adopt the character's point of view sympathetically. So it is necessary, if one plays Carol, to play her sympathetically, to see the play from her point of view. And the same is true if one plays John. One approach that seems to me to be fatal is to think that the play is overbalanced towards John, as many directors argue, and therefore one's job in directing is to redress the balance. This requires inventing fake sympathy for Carol and always rings false. Instead, play her as she is, and understand why she acts as she does; this is equally true for John.

To do this, Mamet would say never be general. Just act the moment, without thinking about where the character might be going next. Thus as the play begins, I would ask, 'What does John do while on the telephone? If I were in that situation, I would be frantically searching for the documents the call refers to regarding the purchase of the house – the easement, etc. Then, trying to get out of the office, I would be putting the papers away as I spoke impatiently to the student – Let's take the mysticism out of it, shall we? [. . .] I'll tell you: when you have some "thing". Which must be broached. (*Pause*) Don't you think . . .? (*Pause*)' (3). He's trying to tell her to get to the point. But then he backs away, apologizes twice for being 'somewhat rushed' in trying to get to this new crisis over the house. From the outset things get off on the wrong foot because she doesn't say what she's come for, her grade, but asks about a 'term of art'.

Similarly Carol must stay in the moment. Try some improvisations to imagine what possibilities there are. What do you do when in someone's office and who is on the telephone on a personal call? Fidget? Reread notes? Pretend to be reading the textbook? Study posters? Get up and look at books on bookcase as if not listening? As director, remember minimalism. Don't clutter the set – but for improvisation or performance the actor may mime these actions. The last production I saw, at the Seaside Repertory Company in Florida, produced bookcovers for John's 'book' so there were twenty copies of his own book on his bookshelves. In my own production one of these books became a useful prop in Act Three for Carol to throw across the room, and for John to pick up lovingly.

As far as John is concerned, however, the play bumps along with his first motivation – finish quickly with the student and get to the house – until page 15 which marks a clear shift. When Carol says she's 'stupid' John seems to feel some kinship with her, and accordingly slows down to explain why he felt stupid as well when he was a student. The passage is strange because he says 'Sit down' five times, 'Please' four times, repeating this over and over until she sits. Is it a confrontation of wills? It is clear that John begging her to stay goes against his own self-interest, ignoring the appeals of his wife and lawyer for the purchase of the house, to work with a student who is in need. Ironically, at the end of the act, he reverses this, and ignores her needs to run off to a surprise party. This is an unexpected yet typical Mamet reversal.

So again, try some improvisations to search for a reason. Why does he keep repeating himself? Why doesn't she sit down? The point of such exercises is that there is no answer to this in the text. One must experiment to find a solution, at least one that works for the two actors involved, and makes sense to the director. One's purpose in performing a play should not be simply to create a *tableau vivant* of the text, a living representation, like illustrations for a children's book which simply depict the words visually. Instead, one's purpose must be to understand the action anew, and find the motivation moment by moment for the character so that an expanded understanding comes to the audience, a recognition they would not get from simply reading the play. Each moment like this allows the actor to produce a momentary glimmer of what the character may be thinking and feeling.

John's feelings are clear until page 24, when Carol blurts, 'I want to know about my grade,' and at that point he offers her the deal to start the course over, and to give her a grade of 'A'. Why would he do this? Again, try improvisation to explore what he could be thinking and feeling at this moment, the turning point for him in the play. If he had not made this offer, the rest of the charges would not have held together. Again, the actor playing Carol should work the improvisation to see how one might react when this offer is made. Then compare her own reaction with Carol's. John never notices this moment, however, and answers her with a canned lecture explaining his view of higher education. This frustrates her until she breaks down when he shifts to 'wring some worth from the statistics' regarding demographics of college-education. When she shouts that she can't understand them, he attempts to console her, and then the final phone call comes summoning him to the surprise party – all the previous calls have been ruses to try to get him to come to the party and leave the student. He finally does.

The end of the first act is the most difficult point in the play for actors and director, to my mind. Debra Eisenstadt told me for her it was the fulcrum of her whole performance, as she begins to confess the secret and then is cut off and ignored by John. How does Carol react after this? What is she to do during his extremely long conversation on the telephone at the end of the act, as she is on the brink of confessing her secret? Again, one must try improvisation to experiment with different reactions. I found through rehearsal the most effective final pose for Brianne Bordes playing Carol, while John was on the telephone, was with her head down between her knees, crying, perhaps, or at least emotionally overwrought and not wanting to be seen.

But after he hangs up, what does she do? Experiment with different possibilities again. Is she simply politely asking him about the call? Is she bitter that he left her in such a vulnerable position? I like the idea of some anger towards him for simply abandoning her to take the call, and then go to the party, without even apologizing to her. He suddenly has no concern for her as a student or as a person – is his mask of concern all a pose? This is implied in the final exchange before the call: 'Why do you want to know this?' 'I don't want to know.' He certainly does not seem to 'want to know', or to be concerned about her. To walk out on a student in the middle of such an emotional breakdown is unforgivable. There are hints he doesn't care, for even as he is lecturing her, he is making notes to himself seeking to avoid paying school taxes while sending his child to a private school. This shows he does not pay any attention even to what he is saying to her at that moment – she is just a lecturing post at that point.

As a result, however, Carol is much more difficult to fathom – for John has most of the words of the Act. One has to start with the premise that she is there to find out how to pass the course, how to improve her grade. But she doesn't get to the point until page 24. Why not? What has she been doing? Before this, however, she makes clear her view of higher education is the opposite of John's. She sees it as dispensing information; he sees it as a place to challenge students to make them rethink their assumptions. In her view, the teacher is a kind of god, someone who 'doesn't forget things' and the responsibility of the student is to take notes, learn what the teacher has to teach. 'I sit in class, I . . . *(She holds up her notebook)* I take notes . . . [. . .] I'm doing what I'm told. I bought your *book*, I read your . . .' (6). On page 9 she repeats this as her mantra: 'I did what you told me. [. . .] I do. . . . Ev . . . [. . .] everything I'm told.' As Perry argues, this is the point of view of at best a 'C' college student. The problem is just doing the work isn't a guarantee of a good grade. And that's her problem: 'No. No. No. I want to understand it' (11). This is what is so frustrating to her. What doesn't she 'understand? (Pause) Any of it. What you're trying to say. When you talk about . . .' (11).

Carol is simply looking for the facts. But John is not teaching facts. And so she cannot understand him. She dances around this frustration until page 14 when she yells at John for the first time: 'WHAT IN THE WORLD ARE YOU *TALKING* ABOUT? And I read your book. And they said, "Fine, go in that class." Because you talked about responsibility to the young. I DON'T KNOW WHAT IT MEANS AND I'M *FAILING* . . .' (14). One needs to experiment here to find the cause of her panic each time it occurs.

The notebook may be a crucial prop, as it was in the Pinter production. In her Tenure Committee report, Carol cites word for word things John said in Act One. So she must be writing down John's words in the first act. In one of my rehearsals Michael Kaffer grabbed the book away from her as John demands she tell him in his own words on page 28. I like that – if not as an action to keep in the production, at least as an indication of his frustration with her inability to speak without notes. An improvisation like this helps to clarify motivation and choices for actors and director.

Most crucial for the play, however, is to find its rhythm. Several actors have observed Mamet as director sitting at rehearsal tapping out iambic pentameter to his lines. Many of the interrupted speeches require precise timing. Rehearse doing speed drills, exchanging lines back and forth as quickly as possible. Get the technique down pat. Many commentators disdain Mamet actors for their staccato-like delivery of lines with very little emotional affect. Yet this is what it takes to get Mamet across – without editorializing or inflection. I would work very hard to drain the performance of emotion – certainly of unnecessary emotion of any kind. Let the audience supply the emotions, and the actors supply the character and lines. Once one has the fast patter stichomythia down pat, figure out where – especially in the first act – one must put on the brakes and both give the audience a rest and slow down because the characters slow down.

In *Act One*, Moss Hart tells the story of his playwriting mentor and partner, cutting the most expensive and funniest scene of their play late in previews. George S. Kaufman had noticed the audience stopped laughing in the middle of it, and decided that, funny as it was, it was too loud, and the audience was too laughed out, and needed a break. It is the same with Mamet's fast back and forth exchanges. Find the moments to slow down. Find the rhythm of each scene and act. In a similar vein to Kaufman, Mamet once remarked that the writer must always throw away his best lines, no matter how hard it is to do. The rhythm is more important. Think of the words as 'gibberish'.

Improvisations and exercises

Improvisation. There are two main reasons for improvisation in rehearsal. First, to put oneself imaginatively into the situation – as in the opening exercises suggested here while John is on the phone. One key to watch for is where one's personal approach to a scene deviates from the direction the character takes. At that point, stop and try to discover why the character goes in this unexpected direction. The second is to explore other options to get one thinking about the situation and exploring various avenues to handle it – as one might at the end of the act with Carol.

Act One
Improvisation 1

The opening sets the audience's relation to the characters. What are they doing and why? What does John do while on the telephone to start the play? One person play John, the other, Grace, his wife, on the telephone. What does she say (that we are not given in the text)? How does John react? What does Carol do while John is talking on the phone? Props? What physical props might one use playing either character? Try a variety as experiments – but ultimately, to be true to Mamet and to keep from absolute realism, try to be minimalist. How does each prop change the meaning of the scene? Does John have a big brief case? Leather? Backpack? Does he have folders with different headings? He needs to find Carol's paper a little later in the scene. Where is that? What does Carol have? Her notes? How carried? The textbook? Does she have a coat on? When does she take it off? How does she collect things to leave in the middle of the scene?

Improvisation 2

Act out going to a professor's office for help in a course. What difference does it make if you are a fact-based student who can't grasp a teacher who offers multiple, conflicting points of view, theories, not answers? How does the teacher change techniques to help such a student? What if the teacher's vocabulary is too specialized for the student to understand?

Improvisation 3

At any point, consider reversing roles/genders. In 1994 my colleague John Hafner did this teaching the play in the Philippines, and the woman playing the teacher found it empowering. Does it make a difference if the teacher is female, the student male? Try this both reading the lines, to see what differences occur, as well as with improvisations. Surprising discoveries can result from this kind of experiment, which can highlight how certain expectations of behaviour are created by gender.

Rhythm – Rapid Line Drills

Actors sometimes practice lines by saying them without expression simply going back and forth as quickly as they can. With playwrights like Pinter and Mamet it is crucial to learn all the lines and cues exactly, because one slight misstep by one actor can cause the other to jump ahead or backwards in the play in response to a similar or identical cue. After that, it is nearly impossible to find one's way back to the right cue. But another function to the rapid line drills is to eliminate the dreaded pauses that directors hate – the director's most constant refrain is, 'pick up the cues'. It means, don't say the words faster, but do cut away the interval between one speaker and another. Concentrate on working especially the ubiquitous ellipses in which one character speaks and then another:

JOHN: Don't you think . . .? (*Pause*)
CAROL: . . . don't I think . . .
JOHN: Mmm?
CAROL: . . . did I . . .?
JOHN: . . . what?
CAROL: Did . . . did I . . . did I say something wr . . .

JOHN: (*Pause*) No. I'm sorry. No. You're right. I'm very sorry. I'm somewhat rushed. (3)

The first thing to notice is that Mamet combines the ellipsis with the (*Pause*) at the start of the exchange, which implies that Carol should not respond right away. It also implies that if he wanted more pauses he would have specified them, so the other speeches should be nearly simultaneous. For this reason the rapid exchange of lines is a good idea as practice. Consider as well the two ways to play these lines. Is Carol taking John to be accusing her of a failure to 'think'? Is he paying any attention to her, or do his muttered responses show he is distracted by the phone conversation which precedes this, and is not thinking about Carol at all? The stichomythic exchanges like this need concentration and a lot of practice at quick picking up of cues. To put in long pauses between each speech would be rather deadly.

Improvisation 4: Page 15

'Sit down.' Try this a variety of ways. Why doesn't Carol sit down when he asks her to? Why does he keep repeating the same words? Is he paying attention? Is she recalcitrant? Does he pull a chair out for her? Try this a variety of ways and with different seating options to find one that makes sense of this curious scene. It is the first turning point – once she sits, she accepts his guidance and expects his help. Why does she at first refuse to sit? Or does she?

Improvisation 5: Pages 36–8

Try out the ending of Act One as an improvisation. One person play the student who is having a breakdown in the office. A terrible secret is about to be confessed. How does the teacher react? How does the student resist yet want to confide the secret? Try this a variety of ways. What kinds of actions by the student would elicit a physical response from the teacher, an attempt to console. How does the student react when touched? This is always a difficult area for student actors – touching another person is always awkward, so one must work through that reluctance to see what works best for the two actors.

Act Two

There are two turning points of power in the scene. Analyse how and why power reverses. The first comes '*simultaneously with* "escalates" ' (48). At this point, Carol takes control and lectures John – first about power, then about gender, then about his teaching style, and finally in a long diatribe on page 52. Break down her arguments. Where does she shift grounds in the long speech and why?

Then John has his long speech on pages 53–4. What is the nature of his argument? Why does Carol lose control to that speech? How does it throw her off the track, or rebut her position? This act is about argumentation, and each takes a position and argues for it. Why does the outcome keep reversing?

Improvisation

Work on the staging of the end of the scene without lines. How does John stop her from leaving? '*He restrains her from leaving*' (57). Try it in action; it has been staged in many different ways. Each ~~~ significant choices. Carol later says of that moment, 'You ~~~ me. I was leaving this office, you "pressed" yourself ~~~d" your body into me' (78). Could she possibly ~~~ he was doing? Later she explains, 'under ~~~ry. [. . .] Yes. And attempted rape. ~~~OED defines it: 'An assailing ~~~tack upon another by beat- ~~~ally the slightest touching of ~~~enacing manner.' Is this too a ~~~il the audience see it if he simply ~~~eaving, versus, for example, putting his hand on the door to keep it shut and pushing against her to do so, versus grabbing her with both hands and pressing himself to restrain her from leaving?

The solution of Lindsay Posner directing Julia Stiles and Aaron Eckhart in the 2005 London production seemed too passive. Eckhart grabbed Stiles' hand and pulled her from the door. There was no basis to the charge of 'attempted assault' no 'you pressed yourself into me' so clearly her charge of rape is complete fabrication and he is total victim. Why deviate in this way from what Mamet has written? Why reconfigure the action of the play? The interpretation doesn't support Carol's view of what happened. This shows how crucial it is to work out what the audience will see in one act, for it forms the basis of the charges in the next.

Last Act

Unlike the first two acts in which Mamet specifies that John and Carol are separated by the desk, here there is no separation: '*At rise, CAROL and JOHN are seated.*' This time she does not allow him to open with a monologue but cuts him off very quickly. The actors then, reflecting the change in costume in which he is dishevelled, she is put together, should experiment with reversal of power in the conversation.

> JOHN: I have asked you here. (*Pause*) I have asked you here against, against my . . .
> CAROL: I was most surprised you asked me.
> JOHN: . . . against my better *judgment*, against . . .
> CAROL: I was most surprised . . .
> JOHN: . . . against the . . . yes. I'm sure.
> CAROL: . . . If you would like me to leave, I'll leave. I'll go right now . . . (*She rises*)
> JOHN: Let us begin *correctly*, may we? I feel . . . (59)

This time it is John who is tentative, and Carol who speaks in sentences. In a two-hander like this it is always useful and interesting to create variety in the rehearsal by reversing the two roles, and that would be especially useful for this play. Let the actor playing Carol do John from another part of the play for a while, and John read Carol's lines. It would help with this scene to understand the power shift as she takes control.

Aside from assertiveness, this reversal of power also alters the sexual dynamic between the two characters, and that too would require some experimentation. He has lost all confidence on how to proceed with her once he is no longer in control.

Carol pounds this point home: 'You want unlimited power. To do and to say what you want. As it pleases you – Testing, Questioning, Flirting . . .'. She reads his remarks to women students from her notes, ('Now, don't *you* look fetching') concluding, 'I saw you, I saw you, Professor. For two semesters sit there, stand there and exploit our, as you thought, "paternal prerogative", and what is that but rape; I swear to God' (66–7). This line is the most problematic in the whole play. Feminists and antifeminists alike object vociferously to the charge of rape here, for it should never be trivialized.

But in the heat of the moment, Carol is carried away into obvious hyperbole, like calling a dictatorial teacher a 'Nazi'. The point is that power, when John had it, allowed him to misuse it with women, not treating them as equals; but similarly Carol, now that she has the power, is equally carried away by it and goes too far, as she does at the end of the scene when she cautions, 'Don't call your wife "baby"' (79). The crossover, in both cases, is from the professional into the personal, without ever realizing what a violation that is.

Carol tries to defuse the sexual, personal dimension of the confrontation when she says, 'I know what you think I am. [. . .] a frightened, repressed, confused, I don't know, abandoned young thing of some doubtful sexuality, who wants, power and revenge'

(68). And once this is acknowledged, she concludes: 'Do you hate me now?' and he admits he does. This is a very gripping moment, one of complete honesty in a play where the characters are so caught up in their roles that they rarely drop the mask. But he cannot make the separation she asks between her as a person, and the role/power she embodies. And she doesn't realize she is now lording the same power over him.

The Stiles/Eckhart production confused this moment. Posner's idea was that as Carol gains power she is more comfortable with her body. But unlike the unisex-dressed Pidgeon, when Stiles said 'You think I'm of some doubtful sexuality' the audience all laughed! Of course, with Julia Stiles, Hollywood starlet, it's already funny; making no effort to neutralize her attractions made it even funnier. Similarly, when he describes himself as pedantic – he wasn't. Macy was, with glasses and academic look. Eckhart, instead, was directed to be someone comfortable with his sexuality, unintentionally opening legs as he leans against desk. He was not flirting, but obliviously male and sexually confident. Posner told the London David Mamet Conference he wanted a younger, sexier professor. Eckhart was in brown cords, and is much more physical an actor than Stiles. But again, the line about 'doubtful sexuality' showed how confusing this direction was.

To elaborate on how power confuses, Carol explains that the sexist language and touching, which he says 'was devoid of sexual content' was not, in her view: 'I say it was not. I SAY IT WAS NOT. Don't you begin to see . . .? Don't you begin to understand? IT'S NOT FOR YOU TO SAY' (70). At this point he begins to back down: 'I take your point. I see there is much good in what you refer to' (71). But John cannot admit to wrongdoing of any kind, and while Carol keeps trying to trap him into an admission of guilt, all he can concede is that he can change . . . but he won't. He never recognizes or accepts any wrongdoing. And he finally returns, once again, to his job. 'What's the use. It's over' (71). Try the lines out in action with her cutting off every move he tries to escape until she literally corners him.

At the end of the play, when Carol presents her list of demands, John suddenly becomes assertive and reverses from the beaten person he was before to rise to a new recognition of his purpose in life:

> I'm sorry. I don't know what I was thinking of. I want to tell you something. I'm a teacher. I am a teacher. Eh? It's my *name* on the door, and I teach the class, and that's what I do. I've got a book with my name on it. And my son will see that book someday. And I have a respon . . . No, I'm sorry . . . I have a *responsibility* . . . to *myself*, to my *son*, to my *profession* . . .. (76)

This list of three items reflects Carol's similar litany earlier in the act: 'I have a responsibility. I . . . [. . .] To? This institution. To the *students*. To my *group*' (65). Notice that Carol leaves out 'myself'. John lists his son, but not his wife nor students, nor to the institution.

The finale has to be the most difficult part of the play to stage. Pinter made the beating much harsher than in Mamet's production. In the film version, Carol fights back at first, pushing John back into a window which breaks the pane. Or rather the pane above where his elbow strikes is what breaks, a continuity blunder. After that, Macy comes stalking her in anger, bleeding from the arm.

Consider what Mamet did in his stage version: John grabs her as she attempts to leave, throws her across the desk lengthwise, knocking everything to the floor, pulls her up while he stands behind his desk, and slaps her twice across the face. Then he punches her in the stomach – she doubles up, and he pushes her completely on top of the desk, rolling over the top of it. He comes around the desk, throws her towards the one side (stage left) chair, then, almost by the hair, throws her towards the bench down right, and she crawls under that bench as he lifts the chair. We hear her panting under the bench. He tucks his shirt in after he puts down the chair, and then goes to straighten his desk before he says, '. . . well . . .' She crawls out just before he says this, stares at him, and, says 'That's right' and takes off her glasses for the last line, said almost to herself, and puts her head down on her arm. Macy's head is now on his arm which rests on the desk.

This requires a lot of rehearsal – no matter how one stages it. Having a stage combat instructor would be the best way to proceed. But again remember that the actions are, essentially, symbolic extensions of the character. So regardless of what looks good, or realistic – the key is to get the audience to think, not to cheer as at a boxing match.

5 Conclusion

The characters, like the setting, are minimalist constructions designed to make the audience fill in the blanks. But when the audience does this, it must realize that the blanks filled become part of the play.

The trick to understanding *Oleanna*, after working through the text and trying out different interpretations in rehearsal or experiment, is to recognize, finally, that the discoveries one makes are more often discoveries of oneself than of Mamet's views. Mamet, as he said to the protesting student at the initial performance, has no answers.

So if on one reading you see Carol as a 'feminazi' inspired by her group, just realize that such a perception is part of the ideology our culture programs us with, rather than part of the play. If one sympathizes with John for losing his job, his family, his home – those middle class fears are highlighted in the play. The play is designed to work on a partially subconscious level – the level of fears. 'I'm as angry, scared, and confused as the rest of you. I don't have the answers' (Holmberg, 1992: 94). The fears Mamet details, however, are the nightmares of our 'National Dream-Life': 'We respond to a drama to that extent to which it corresponds to our dream life. The life of the play is the life of the unconscious, the protagonist represents ourselves, and the main action of the play constitutes the subject of the dream or myth' (8).

Mamet's work on stage and film before and after *Oleanna* (1992) reflects the techniques highlighted here. The previous play, *Speed-the-Plow* (1988), features another female character who is almost a cipher. Reviewers raked Madonna over the coals as a failure with no stage presence when she premiered the role, not realizing that she was doing perfect Mamet acting. It took seeing subsequent actors in the role, Felicity Huffman who succeeded her in New York, and Rebecca Pidgeon in London, to bring about the recognition that the character is designed for the audience to fill in the gap, on which they might project their fears. The plays after *Oleanna* are more autobiographical, but *Cryptogram* (1995) and *The Old Neighborhood* (1997) similarly feature blank characters like the boy John and Bobby Gould whose characters audiences have to extrapolate because there are few speeches giving particulars about their lives.

In film, Mamet's most Hitchcockian works, *The House of Games* (1987) and *The Spanish Prisoner* (1998), invite the audience to enter into the fiction itself, to be misled, tricked by the endings of both works, for a more entertaining purpose than with *Oleanna*. But Mamet's subsequent work has never explored quite as directly the 'National Dream-Life' fears as *Oleanna*. Instead, he seems to have worked on his craft in writing genre plays and films, as if moving away from *Oleanna* which may have cut too close to the bone, raising emotions and issues beyond the playwright's control.

It is difficult to find a play which burrows as deeply into the audience's subconscious, or one that raised more insecurities about power, teacher over student, male over female. And by reversing these power positions, *Oleanna* managed to reveal deep fears within the culture.

Even more significantly, perhaps, it raises the spectre of postmodern instability in a dramatic form. The play takes Mamet's desire to engage the audience to the extreme of discussion, confrontation, and argument lasting long after the performance. It is a play, as a result, which overflows the boundaries between art and life with much the same effect as Ibsen's *A Doll's House* did more than one hundred years before when modern drama began. The difference is that Ibsen's play quite clearly takes sides, and privileges Nora over Torwald. Mamet's desire, at least, in *Oleanna*, is to bring the audience beyond that position of certitude to a position of instability, to see the play from both points of view rather than from just one. Yet even as one articulates why one point of view should be privileged, the polarities reverse, and one can see the play from the opposite point of view. Like the Anita Hill/Clarence Thomas confrontation, two people can see the same incident with totally different optics. Yet the resolution to such a predicament cannot simply be that the side with the most power wins. That is the problem the play most clearly reveals – to be in power creates unconscious blinders to the other person.

The earliest books on Mamet, Christopher Bigsby's and Dennis Carroll's, both took the view that Mamet was in fact a moralistic writer. Carroll sees beyond the tough-guy image 'a moralist who passionately believes in the theatre's power for communion' (1987: 3). Bigsby rejects those who see the externals, speech patterns and realism, seeing instead:

A Moralist lamenting the collapse of public form and private purpose, exposing a spiritually desiccated world in which the cadences of despair predominate, and the occasional consonance offered by relationship or the momentary lyricism buried deep inside the structure of language implies little more than an echo of what was once a state of grace. (1985: 15)

In *Oleanna*, though written somewhat later and in a style new to Mamet, some of the same tensions can be seen. The utopia of higher education may have flipped over into dystopia for now, but the ideal is not dead. Mamet's purpose, as in 'A National Dream Life' has been to remove the blinders from society, to bring the audience to confront what it has repressed. In the process, we must all come to realize 'We can only interpret the behavior of others through the screen we . . . create' and as a consequence come to see from another's perspective as well as our own. This is the only way to discover the lost state of grace, the utopia hidden by dystopia.

Timeline

Political

1986 Ronald Reagan privatizes financing of higher education as a young person's investment in future – student loans replace government grants: 'I believe this project, which allows borrowers to finance more of their own college costs more easily out of their long-term earnings, may signal an important, new direction in the financing of postsecondary education.'

1982 to 1990 Clarence Thomas Chairman of the US Equal Employment Opportunity Commission

1987 Dow Jones Industrial Average falls 22.6 per cent in single session on Black Monday

1987 Margaret Thatcher wins third term

1989 Students are massacred in China's Tiananmen Square

1989 The Berlin Wall, the border separating Western and Eastern

Social

1987 Film: *Fatal Attraction*. Rejected lover refuses to give up. She pursues her married lover

1987 Stephen King's novel *Misery*; film 1990. Ex-nurse imprisons injured novelist

1988 Mamet, *Speed-the-Plow*. Secretary tries to get Hollywood producer to film a serious work

1988 Wendy Wasserstein, *Heidi Chronicles*. Twenty years in the life of a feminist art scholar

1988 Hwang, *M. Butterfly*. Twenty years' affair of French diplomat with a man he thinks is a woman

1991 Tony Kushner's *Angels in America*, London, Royal National Theatre. Sexual orientation and gender issues play against the political backdrop of the 1980s

1991 Susan Faludi, *Backlash: The Undeclared War Against American Women*

Political

Germany is torn down. The fall of the Berlin Wall will always be seen as a symbol for the end of the Cold War

1990 Iraq invades Kuwait leading to 1991 Gulf War

1991 September Tailhook Convention of Navy Pilots results in sexual assaults

1991 On 11 October, Anita Hill is summoned to testify before the Senate Judiciary Committee hearings on the confirmation of Clarence Thomas

1992 Clinton elected

1993 Lorena Bobbitt chops off her husband's penis as he lies sleeping in their Virginia home. She then drives off with it and flings it out of her car window. Police search and locate it, and it is then surgically reattached

1995 O. J. Simpson acquitted of murder of wife

1996 Clinton is re-elected

1995–96 Monica Lewinsky is an intern with President Clinton. He admits to having a sexual relationship with her. This leads to

Social

1991 Anna Deavere Smith, *Fires in the Mirror*. Multiple perspectives on race riot in New York; Smith plays all the roles based on interviews

1992 Kushner's *Angels in America*, New York

1994 Michael Crichton's Novel and Film *Disclosure*: worker is sued for sexual harassment by a former lover turned boss who initiated the act forcefully, which threatens both his career and his personal life

1994 Mamet, *Cryptogram*, Premier London

1996 Mark Ravenhill's *Shopping and F***ing*, Royal Court Theatre, London

1997 Patrick Marber, *Closer*, Royal National Theatre, London

1997 Mamet, *Old Neighborhood* Premier NewYork

1997 Paula Vogel, *How I Learned to Drive*, Uncle's sexual abuse of niece. Vineyard Theater, NewYork

Political

the impeachment of Clinton and the
surrounding scandals of 1997–99

1997 Tony Blair elected Labour
Prime Minister

1997 Princess Diana dies in car crash

Further Reading

Editions

Mamet, David (1993), *Oleanna*. New York: Vintage Books. The common US paperback edition, used as the text in this book's citations.

Oleanna. Dir. David Mamet. Samuel Goldwyn Co., 1994. [film] DVD released 27 June 1995 Hallmark Entertainment.

David Mamet Plays: 4. (2002) London: Methuen. Collected works volume.

Rosenthal, Daniel. (2004), *Oleanna: Methuen Student Edition with Commentary & Notes*. London: Methuen. Focuses on the London production.

Playwright

Leslie Kane's (1999), *Weasels and Wisemen* examines Mamet's ethical and religious dimension, explains Jewish background, and notes the 'minimalist dialogue' as key to *Oleanna*. Christopher Bigsby's *The Cambridge Companion to David Mamet* (2004) has an excellent selection of essays on Mamet's works. For the words of Mamet himself, Leslie Kane's anthology, *David Mamet in Conversation* is the easiest introduction to his thoughts, as are his books of essays – especially *Writing in Restaurants* (1986). Kane also compiled an excellent anthology of scholarly essays with Christopher Hudgins in 2001, *Gender and Genre: Essays on David Mamet*.

Play

Brenda Murphy (2004), provides a very complete overview of scholarly interpretations of *Oleanna*. In addition, she has her own unique reading of the ending as a balanced recognition of Carol and John (*The Cambridge Companion to David Mamet*, 124–38). Robert Skloot's (2001) '*Oleanna*, or, the Play of Pedagogy' (*Gender and Genre*, 95–109) is the best essay on using the play to examine 'how we can teach and learn better' (104).

More stridently, Carla McDonough, in *Staging Masculinity* (1997), takes Mamet to task as she fills in gaps and constructs Carol as 'a vicious harpy out to destroy her professor's livelihood, life and soul. Her penchant for wilfully misunderstanding John's well intentioned, if highly befuddled, gestures and words provides a convincing argument that sexual harassment charges are bogus and that political correctness is to blame for disrupting an otherwise comfortable, if somewhat paternalistic, system' (96). The hyperbole here, depicting Carol as out to destroy John's 'soul' indicates the degree to which the writer has filled in a scenario of her own. Katherine Burkman (1998) similarly is a noted Mamet-basher; she has an essay on how Pinter redeemed the play from anti-feminist Mamet.

Postmodernism and social background

Paul Berman's anthology, *Debating P. C.* (1992), is the most timely introduction to the issues of political correctness which *Oleanna* addresses. On the recoil against feminism in the time, see Susan Faludi's *Backlash* (1991). For a general background to American culture and drama, the best surveys are Christopher Bigsby's (2000) *Modern American Drama, 1945–2000* and Matthew Roudané's (1997) *American Drama Since 1960*.

The major theorists of postmodernism, especially in its literary incarnation, are Lyotard (1984) and Jameson (1991). Linda Hutcheon applied the theory to literature (1988). Stephen Watt (1998) supplies the most extended application to drama in *Postmodern/Drama*. He observes that earlier modern drama 'was strongly influenced by notions of subjective depth' (23). By contrast, Watt argues that in contemporary plays human subjectivity is defined by breadth, so it has to be examined in a larger artistic, political and economic context than was necessary with the depth model in which character itself was the basis of analysis. For a specific application, Thomas Porter (2000) examines 'Postmodernism and Violence in Mamet's *Oleanna*'.

References

Videotape

David Mamet: The Playwright as Director (1979), Videotape. Kent, CT: Creative Arts Television.

Books/Journal articles

Althusser, Louis (1971), 'Ideology and Ideological State Apparatuses', in *Lenin and Philosophy and Other Essays* (trans. Ben Brewster). London: NLB. Rpt. in Julie Rivkin and Michael Ryan (eds), *Literary Theory: An Anthology*. Oxford: Blackwell, 1998, pp. 294–304.

Badenhausen, Richard (1998), 'The Modern Academy Raging in the Dark: Misreading Mamet's Political Incorrectness in *Oleanna*', *College Literature* 25.3, 1–19.

Barbour, David (1993), 'Academic Gowns [Oleanna Costumes]', *TCI* 27.3 March, 8.

Barnes, Clive (1992), 'Mamet with a Thud', *New York Post* 26 October. Rpt. in *New York Theatre Critics' Reviews* 53.19, p. 359.

Bauer, Dale M. (1998), 'Indecent Proposals: Teachers in the Movies', *College English* 60. 3, 301–17.

Bean, Kellie (2001), 'A Few Good Men: Collusion and Violence in *Oleanna*', in Christopher C. Hudgins and Leslie Kane (eds), *Gender and Genre: Essays on David Mamet*. New York: Palgrave, pp. 109–25.

Bechtel, Roger (1996), 'P. C. Power Play: Language and Representation in David Mamet's *Oleanna*', *Theatre Studies* 41, 29–48.

Berman, Paul (1992), *Debating P. C.: The Controversy Over Political Correctness on College Campuses*. New York: Laurel Dell.

Bigsby, Christopher (1985), *David Mamet*. London and New York: Methuen.

—(2000), *Modern American Drama, 1945–2000*. Cambridge: CUP.

—(2004), *The Cambridge Companion to David Mamet*. Cambridge: CUP.

Braun, Heather (2004), 'The 1990s', in Christopher Bigsby (ed.), *Cambridge Companion to David Mamet*. Cambridge: Cambridge University Press, pp. 103–23.

Burkman, Katherine H. (1998), 'The Web of Misogyny in Mamet and Pinter's Betrayal Games', in Burkman and Judith Roof (eds), *Staging the Rage: The Web of Misogyny in Modern Drama*. Cranbury, NJ: Associated University Presses, pp. 27–38.

Carroll, Dennis (1987), *Modern Dramatists: David Mamet*. New York: St. Martin's.

Cohn, Ruby (1995), *Anglo–American Interplay in Recent Drama*. Cambridge: Cambridge UP.

Committee on the Judiciary of the United States Senate (1991), *Nomination of Judge Clarence Thomas to be Associate Justice of the Supreme Court of the United States*. 11–13 October. Part 4 of 4 Parts. Washington: US Govt. Printing Office, 1993.

Dunbar-Odom, Donna (2003), 'Resistance and Authority; Film as a Tool to Train Teachers', *The Composition Forum* 14.1, 17–31.

Ebert, Roger (1994), 'On "*Oleanna*": The Play's the Thing – Film Can't Cut It', *Chicago Sun-Times* 4 November, Weekend 26.

Elam, Harry J., Jr. (1997), '"Only in America": Contemporary American Theater and the Power of Performance', in Marc Maufort (ed.), *Voices of Power: Co-Operation and Conflict in English Language and Literatures*. Liège, Belgium: English Dept., Univ. of Liège, pp. 151–63.

Faludi, Susan (1991), *Backlash*: The Undeclared War Against American Women. New York: Crown.

Feingold, Michael (1992), 'Prisoners of Unsex', *Village Voice* 3 Nov., 109. Rpt. in *New York Theatre Critics' Reviews* 53.19, 357.

Fish, Stanley (1992), 'There's No Such Thing as Free Speech, and It's a Good Thing, Too', in Paul Berman (ed.), *Debating P. C.: The Controversy Over Political Correctness on College Campuses*. New York: Bantam Laurel Dell, pp. 231–45.

Foster, Verna (1995), 'Sex, Power, and Pedagogy in Mamet's *Oleanna* and Ionesco's *The Lesson*', *American Drama* 5.1, 36–50.

Fraser, Gerald (1976), 'Mamet's Plays Shed Masculinity Myth', *New York Times* 5 July, A7.

Garner, Stanton B. Jr. (2000), 'Framing the Classroom: Pedagogy, Power, *Oleanna*', *Theatre Topics* 10.1, 9–59.

Goggans, Thomas H. (1997), 'Laying Blame: Gender and Subtext in David Mamet's Oleanna', *Modern Drama* 40.3, 433–41.

Hansen, Liane, William Macy and Debra Eisenstadt (1993), 'David Mamet's *Oleanna* Raises Questions of Harassment', 2 May National Public Radio Weekend Edition [transcript on Lexis/Nexis].

Hardin, Miriam (1999), 'Lessons from the Lesson: Four Post-Ionescan Education Plays', *CEA Magazine: A Journal of the College English Association*, Middle Atlantic Group 12, 30–46.

'He Said . . . She Said . . . Who Did What?' (1992), *New York Times* 15 November, H6.

Henry III, William A. (1992), 'Reborn with Relevance', *Time* 2 Nov., 69. Rpt. in *New York Theatre Critics' Reviews* 53.19, 363.

Holmberg, Arthur (1992), 'Approaches: The Language of Misunderstanding', *American Theatre* 9.6, 94–5.

Hudgins, Christopher C. and Leslie Kane (eds) (2001), *Gender and Genre: Essays on David Mamet*. New York: Palgrave.

Hutcheon, Linda (1988), *Poetics of Postmodernism: History, Theory, Fiction*. New York and London: Routledge.

Isaacs, Jeremy (1998), 'Face to Face', BBC2 Interview, 23 Feb., in Leslie Kane (ed.), *David Mamet in Conversation*. Ann Arbor: Univ. of Michigan Press, pp. 211–25.

Jameson, Frederic (1991), *Postmodernism: Or, The Cultural Logic of Late Capitalism*. Durham: Duke Univ. Press.

Kane, Leslie (1999), *Weasels and Wisemen: Ethics and Ethnicity in the Work of David Mamet*. New York: St. Martin's Press.

Keroes, Jo (1999), *Tales Out of School: Gender, Longing, and the Teacher in Fiction and Film*. Carbondale, IL: Southern Illinois UP.

Kroll, Jack (1992), 'A Tough Lesson in Sexual Harassment', *Newsweek* 9 Nov., 65. Rpt. in *New York Theatre Critics' Reviews* 53.19, 360.

Lahr, John (1992), 'Dogma Days', *New Yorker* 16 Nov., 121+. Rpt. in *New York Theatre Critics' Reviews* 53.19, 351–3.

Lazare, Lewis (2007), 'Mamet Goes Commercial', *Chicago Sun-Times* 4 May, 59.

Lyotard, Jean-François (1984), *The Postmodern Condition: A Report on Knowledge*. Trans. Geoff Bennington and Brian Massumi. Minneapolis: Univ. of Minnesota Press.

MacLeod, Christine (1995), 'The Politics of Gender, Language, and Hierarchy in Mamet's *Oleanna*', *Journal of American Studies* 29.2, 199–213.

Mamet, David (1974), 'Stanislavsky and Squirrels', *Chicago Sun-Times* 6 October, sec. 3.

—(1986), *Writing in Restaurants*. New York: Viking.

—(1986), 'A National Dream-Life', *Writing in Restaurants*. New York: Viking, pp. 8–11.

—(1986), 'Radio Drama', *Writing in Restaurants*. New York: Viking, pp. 12–18.

—(1988), *Homicide*. New York: Grove.

—(1989), *Some Freaks*. New York: Viking.

—(1991), *On Directing Film*. New York: Viking.

—(1992), *The Cabin*. New York: Turtle Bay.

—(1993), *Oleanna*. New York: Vintage.

—(1993), 'Mamet on Playwriting', *The Dramatists Guild Quarterly* 30 (Spring), 10.

—(1996), *Make-Believe Town*. New York: Little, Brown.

—(1997), *True and False: Heresy and Common Sense for the Actor*. New York: Pantheon.

—(1999), 'Salad Days', *Jafsie and John Henry: Essays*. New York: Free Press, pp. 8–11.

—(2001), *David Mamet in Conversation*. Leslie Kane (ed.). Ann Arbor: University of Michigan Press.

—(2002), *South of the Northeast Kingdom*. Washington, DC: National Geographic.

Marvin, Blanche (1993), Rev. of *Oleanna*. *London Theatre Reviews 42/43* (June/July) 17.

Mason, David V. (2001), 'The Classical American Tradition: Meta-Tragedy in *Oleanna*', *Journal of American Drama and Theatre* 13.3, 55–72.

McDermott, James Dishon (2006), *Austere Style in Twentieth-Century Literature: Literary Minimalism*. Lewiston, NY: Edward Mellen Press, pp. 115–45.

McDonough, Carla (1997), *Staging Masculinity: Male Identity in Contemporary American Drama*. Jefferson, NC and London: McFarland.

Murphy, Brenda (2004), '*Oleanna*: Language and Power', in Christopher Bigsby (ed.), *Cambridge Companion to David Mamet*. Cambridge: Cambridge UP, pp.124–38.

Norman, Geoffrey and John Rezak. (1995), 'Working the Con', *Playboy* April, 51+, in Leslie Kane's *David Mamet in Conversation*. Ann Arbor: Univ. of Michigan Press, pp. 123–42.

Perry, William G. Jr. (1970), *Forms of Intellectual and Moral Development in the College Years: A Scheme*. New York: Holt, Rinehart.

Piette, Alain (1995), 'The Devil's Advocate: David Mamet's *Oleanna* and Political Correctness', in Marc Maufort (ed.), *Staging Difference: Cultural Pluralism in American Theatre and Drama,* Theatre Arts 25. New York: Peter Lang, pp. 173–87.

Porter, Thomas E. (2000), 'Postmodernism and Violence in Mamet's *Oleanna*', *Modern Drama* 43.1, 13–32.

Raymond, Richard C. (2003), 'Rhetoricizing English Studies: Students' Ways of Reading *Oleanna*', *Pedagogy* 3.1, 53–72.

Rich, Frank (1992), 'Mamet's New Play Detonates the Fury of Sexual Harassment', *New York Times* 26 Oct., B1+, in *Hot Seat.* New York: Random House 1998, pp. 907–9.

Richards, David (1992), 'The Jackhammer Voice of Mamet's "*Oleanna*"', *New York Times* 8 Nov., sec. 2: 1.

—(1993), 'Mamet's Women: From Wimp to Warrior', *New York Times* 3 Jan., sec. B: 1+.

Rose, Charlie (1994), 'On Theater, Politics, and Tragedy', Interview on the 'Charlie Rose Show', WNET, 11 Nov., in Leslie Kane (ed.), *David Mamet in Conversation.* Ann Arbor: Univ. of Michigan Press, pp. 163–81.

Rosenfeld, Megan (1993), 'Exit Audience, Arguing: A Poll on Mamet's Uneven Battle of the Sexes', *Washington Post* 30 April, B1.

Rosenthal, Daniel (2004), *Oleanna: Methuen Student Edition with Commentary and Notes.* London: Methuen.

Roudané, Matthew (1997), *American Drama Since 1960: A Critical History.* Boston: Twayne.

Russo, Francine (1993), 'Mamet's Traveling Cockfight', *Village Voice* 29 June, 96.

Rutherford, Malcolm (1993), Rev. of *Oleanna. Financial Times* 2 July. Rpt. in *Theatre Record* 18 June–1 July, 742.

Ryan, Stephen (1996), 'Oleanna: David Mamet's Power Play', *Modern Drama* 39.3, 392–403.

Sauer, David Kennedy and Janice A. (2003), *David Mamet: A Resource and Production Sourcebook*. London and Westport, Connecticut: Praeger.

—(2000), '*Oleanna* and *The Children's Hour*: Misreading Sexuality on the Post/Modern Realistic Stage', *Modern Drama* 43.3, 421–40. Rpt. in Harold Bloom, et al. (eds), *David Mamet*. New York: Chelsea House, 2004, pp. 203–25.

Schvey, Henry I. (1988), 'Celebrating the Capacity for Self-Knowledge', *New Theatre Quarterly* 4.13, 89–96, in Leslie Kane (ed.), *David Mamet in Conversation*. Ann Arbor: Univ. of Michigan Press, pp. 60–71.

Shipton, Geraldine (2007), 'The Annihilation of Triangular Space in David Mamet's *Oleanna* and Some Implications for Teacher–Student Relationships in the Era of Mass University Education', *Psychodynamic Practice* 13. 2 May, 141–52.

Shulgasser, Barbara (1998), 'Mountebanks and Misfits', in Leslie Kane (ed.), *David Mamet in Conversation*. Ann Arbor: Univ. of Michigan Press, pp. 192–210.

Sierz, Aleks (1993), Rev. of *Oleanna*. *Tribune* [UK] 9 July. Rpt. in *Theatre Record* 18 June–1 July, 740.

Silverstein, Marc (1992), '"We're Just Human": *Oleanna* and Cultural Crisis', *South Atlantic Review* 60.2, 103–20.

Simon, John (1992), 'Thirteen Ways of Looking at a Turkey', *New York* 9 Nov., 72. Rpt. in *New York Theatre Critics' Reviews* 53.19, 361–2.

Skloot, Robert (2001), '*Oleanna*, or the Play of Pedagogy', in Christopher Hudgins and Leslie Kane (eds), *Gender and Genre: Essays on David Mamet*. New York: Palgrave, pp. 95–109.

Solomon, Alisa (1992), 'Mametic Phallacy', *Village Voice* 24 Nov.,104. Rpt. in *New York Theatre Critics' Reviews* 53.19, 355–6.

Stayton, Richard (1992), 'Then He Created Woman', *Newsday* 25 Oct., sec. Funfair: 7+.

Sterritt, David (1992), 'Drama Touches on Political Power', *Christian Science Monitor* 30 Oct.,12. Rpt. in *New York Theatre Critics' Reviews* 53.19, 358.

Stuart, Jan (1992), 'Mamet's Reactionary Howl on Sexual Harassment', *Newsday* 26 Oct. Rpt. in *New York Theatre Critics' Reviews* 53.19, 356.

Taylor, Paul (1993), 'Dramatically Incorrect', *Independent* 2 July, sec. Arts: 15. Rpt. in *Theatre Record* 18 June–1 July, 743.

Vorlicky, Robert (2005), 'Keynote Address', Second Conference of the David Mamet Society, London, June.

Watt, Douglas (1992), Rev. of *Oleanna*. *Daily News* [New York] 30 Oct. Rpt. in *New York Theatre Critics' Reviews* 53.19, 360.

Watt, Stephen (1998), *Postmodern/Drama: Reading the Contemporary Stage*. Ann Arbor: Univ. of Michigan Press.

Weales, Gerald (1992), 'Gender Wars', *Commonweal* 4 Dec., 15+.

Weber, Bruce (1992), 'On Stage and Off', *New York Times* 30 Oct., C2.

Weber, Jean Jacques (1998), 'Three Models of Power in David Mamet's *Oleanna*', in Jonathan Culpeper, et al. (eds), *Exploring the Language of Drama: From Text to Context*. New York: Routledge, pp. 112–27.

Weiskind, Ron (1994), '"*Oleanna*": Lost on Film, So to Speak', *Pittsburgh Post-Gazette* 7 Dec., B6.

Wolf, Matt (1993), 'London *Oleanna* Deepens the Debate', *American Theatre* Nov., 77–8.

Worthen, William (1999), *The Rhetoric of Modern Drama*. Cambridge: Cambridge UP.

Zeifman, Hersh (1994), Rev. of *Oleanna*. *David Mamet Review* 1, 2–3.

Zweigler, Mark (1976), 'Solace of a Playwright's Ideas', in Leslie Kane's *David Mamet in Conversation*. Ann Arbor: Univ. of Michigan Press, 2001, pp. 16–21.

Index